To my mother Rabia who left a legacy behind…

The Timeless Journey

A percentage of profits from the sale of *Fusion* will be contributed to the Hadj Campaign launched by the author.

The funds thus collected will enable us to finance the Hadj Pilgrimage of a number of deserving pilgrims who are unable to afford the cost of this sacred journey.

The Hadj Campaign successfully sent nine pilgrims in 2008 from national regions and was assisted by various community businesses as well as by the community itself. The profits of the recipe book *Indulge* were used to cover accommodation and other essential expenses of the pilgrims who were recipients of the tickets. In 2009 the Hadj Campaign held hands with Channel Islam International Radio Station and send two pilgrims for their sacred pilgrimage.

It is this concept that has rendered the entire project a blessed one and we are privileged once again to look forward to the success of an idea that is dedicated to a sacred and virtuous purpose. The Hadj Campaign is a non-profit organisation and it is there for the benefit of the community only.

No Board Members benefit from this project, directly or indirectly, as it is entirely voluntary.

All nominations to be forwarded to:
P.O. Box 117, Retreat 7965
info@hadjsa.co.za
www.hadjsa.co.za

Fusion

East meets West

SHANAAZ PARKER

SUNBIRD PUBLISHERS

SUNBIRD PUBLISHERS

The illustrated imprint of Jonathan Ball Publishers

First published in 2005
Revised Edition 2009
This edition published in 2011

Sunbird Publishers (Pty) Ltd
P O Box 6836
Roggebaai 8012
Cape Town, South Africa

www.sunbirdpublishers.co.za

Registration number: 1984/003543/07

Design and typesetting by MR Design
Cover design by MR Design
Editing and project management by Michelle Marlin
Proofreading by Kathy Sutton
Photography and styling by Christoph and Diane Heierli, and Mohammed Jaffer
Styling assistant: Alexia Kondylis
Props supplied by @home, Tessa Sonik, Aldona Fine Linen
Cover reproduction by Resolution Colour (Pty) Ltd, Cape Town
Printed and bound by Imago Productions (FE) Pte Ltd, Singapore

www.shanaazparkercooking.com

ISBN 978-1-920289-44-7

Contents

Author ACKNOWLEDGEMENTS

I am thankful to the Almighty for granting me the strength and knowledge, enabling me to offer my best.

My deep gratitude goes to my children Zunaid and Rehana, my brothers, sister, brother– and sisters–in–law and my extended family. An abiding gratitude is owed to dear friends, students and the many wonderful people who use my recipes for their constant love, encouragement, motivation and patience. Without your support and that of Rukeya Ebrahim and Naseema Allie, my dear friends and colleagues, I would never have been able to complete this book.

A special thank you to the cooks for always trying out the new recipes and for cooking up a storm at the Shanaaz Parker Student Residence.

To Ayesha Mathews for all the typing and re–typing, Lameez Jeearry for all the driving, dropping and picking up. You were fast on your wheels.

To my publisher Ceri for trusting, believing and knowing that this is the right book to accept, Michelle my project coordinator, Marius my layout designer,

Kathy my proofreader and Diane and Christoph my photographers: I salute you for your exceptional skill as artists and managers.

To all of those people who have worked on the previous edition of this recipe book, I thank you graciously for your contributions. We have done it again!

To Mahmood Sanglay for providing the editorial support for a project that needed the balance of technical and creative expertise.

To Fatima Allie for seeing exactly what I believed in.

Last, but not least, to my brother Hoosain Narker who always said, 'I don't have the time, but we have to do it now'.

The constancy in prayer, blessings and support from all of the above are part of everything good and virtuous in this book.

I am truly blessed.

Shanaaz Parker

Foreword

This book reflects the passion, dedication and experience of Shanaaz Parker in her journey to achieve excellence in the culinary arts. These are indeed the same attributes she applied in her responsibilities as Head of The School of Cooking during my years as Rector at the Athlone Technical College.

The standards the author strives for are not limited to delicious food, but also extend to appealing presentation, optimal nutritional value and education.

However, the most striking feature of the book is the ease and success with which it achieves the celebrated 'fusion' of culinary traditions. In a South African context this is particularly significant because of the diversity we all have learned to embrace in our country over the past decade. The sense of pride and the freedom to express oneself in a given culture, together with the capacity to respect other cultures is the foundation for any kind of cultural fusion. Furthermore, the book is founded on Shanaaz Parker's involvement with the community and her efforts to develop the skills of our youth as the basis for sound family values.

The contents tempt the taste buds, but also contribute to the knowledge base in the culinary industry. In this sense the book shares knowledge on a publishing platform that has in our years of disparity been inaccessible to both the author and readers.

Finally, given that the contents have been developed from generations of traditional cuisine transformed into fusion food, there is clearly the enduring appeal of the best of the old and the new. I look forward to enjoying every delightful offering!

Leon Beech
Chief Executive Officer
Northlink College

Introduction

South Africa, often spoken of as the 'Rainbow Nation', has a rich and diverse make–up of people coming from many parts of the world. All our people and their cultures have certainly influenced South African cuisine. For example, the Malay and Indian communities have made a rich and distinctive contribution to the diverse South African palate.

Conversely, in the larger context of cultural assimilation, both Indian and Malay cuisines have been subject to typically African and South African influences. It is this wonderfully rich blend of cuisines produced in the cross–cultural landscape of South Africa from which this book draws its sources, some of which come from places and people in both East and West, even beyond the respective communities' countries or origin.

In the spirit of multiculturalism that is a hallmark of South African life after more than a decade of democracy, we embrace the diversity of our people in many ways. One way – and a very personal and intrinsic way – is the food that we eat. Therefore, the contents of this book reflect a discerning selection of the best of old–time traditional and classical recipes.

This presented me with the opportunity to add a 'twist' which infuses the recipes with new life. It is in this sense that the recipes, the food styling and selection may truly be called 'Fusion Food' – a label that is applied to merging and hybridisation of elements of culture. In the culinary arts, this is particularly applicable to ingredients, presentation and distinctive flavour.

But no matter what it's called, it's a celebration of the food that we eat today and the delight it offers the palate as many cultures meet on a single plate. In all the innovation of multicultural food, there has been no compromise on health, presentation, convenience and the enduring appeal of really good food.

The book is intended as an answer to the all too familiar chore of what to cook next, with a range of interesting and tasty meals. This book will provide you with recipes and ideas that will not only inspire you to cook, but will also satisfy those for whom you are cooking. Remember, all cooks are influenced and taught by other cooks and we are no exception.

Enjoy and have fun!

Shanaaz Parker

Getting the Best
OUT OF THIS BOOK

Variety may be the spice of life, but simplicity is certainly the way to get the best of East and West. Ingredients used in the recipes in this book are all indigenous – we already have them on our supermarket shelves and in our kitchens. We all have jeera, koljana, chilli powder and turmeric in our spice drawers. We all have rice, pasta, lentils, and chutney in our pantries. Fresh crispy salad leaves, crunchy apples, cucumbers, peppers, firm tomatoes and the like are all readily available at the nearest shops.

No difficult cooking or baking techniques are required. Techniques or methods that our moms, grandmothers and aunts taught us are what this book places emphasis on. Remember though, that all measuring for baking must be level. Use the measuring cups and spoons that belong to the same set. Do not mix cups and spoons from different sets as this will affect your baking results. Read all recipes carefully and make sure that you understand them. Get all ingredients together.

Cooking instructions are easy to follow. All recipes are good tempered and few need lots of attention. Certain dishes may be made in advance and they can be refrigerated and frozen successfully. The spice quantities given are a guide – you may increase or decrease the quantities should you want a dish to be more or less spicy. Most recipes require slow cooking which enhances their flavour. On refrigeration, the flavour of most dishes tends to improve.

The limited time and pressure of life today compels us to pack the most into our 24 hours. Here is a cook book that provides one with the opportunity to create delectable dishes on a daily basis. Meals may be planned in advance for variety and nutritional value. The following tables respectively indicate the traditional and corresponding English names of the most common spices and offer a guide for imperial and metric conversions in measuring ingredients.

SPICE CHART

INDIAN NAME	ENGLISH NAME
JEERA	CUMIN
KOLJANA	CORIANDER SPICE
BORRIE	TURMERIC
BARISHAP	FENNEL
DHANIA	FRESH CORIANDER
CHILLI POWDER	CAYENNE PEPPER

PERFECT RICE

Grams versus cups and yields

1 kg white rice	= 5 cups raw	= 15 cups cooked	= 15 – 18 portions
1 cup raw rice	= 200 grams	= 3 cups cooked rice	= 2 – 3 portions

To cook rice

ABSORPTION METHOD

1 cup rice requires 2 cups water – for absorption method.

Approx. 10 minutes cooking time

STEAMING METHOD

1 cup rice requires 4 cups water – for boiling, strain water off, then steam.

Approx. 12 minutes cooking time

Conversion CHARTS

Imperial	Metric
¼ teaspoon	1 ml
½ teaspoon	2 ml
¾ teaspoon	4 ml
1 teaspoon	5 ml
1 tablespoon	15 ml
⅕ cup	50 ml
¼ cup	65 ml
⅓ cup	85 ml
⅖ cup	100 ml
½ cup	125 ml
⅗ cup	150 ml
⅔ cup	170 ml
¾ cup	190 ml
⅘ cup	200 ml
1 cup	250 ml

Metric	Imperial
15 g	½ oz
30 g	1 oz
60 g	2 oz
90 g	3 oz
125 g	4 oz
150 g	5 oz
180 g	6 oz
210 g	7 oz
250 g	8 oz (½ pound)
500 g	1 pound
1 kg	2 pounds
300 ml	½ pint
600 ml	1 pint
1,25 litres	2 pint

Note: ml cannot be converted to grams, i.e. 1 cup flour = 250 ml flour = 120 g
Always use measuring spoons, measuring cups and a kitchen scale.

Oven conversion chart

°C	°F	Oven
100	200	very cool
140	275	cool
150	300	cool
160	325	moderately cool
180	350	moderate
190	375	moderately hot
200	400	hot
220	425	very hot
230	450	extremely hot
240	475	extremely hot
260	500	extremely hot
280	550	extremely hot

Checklist
OF KITCHEN EQUIPMENT

SMALL KITCHEN EQUIPMENT

APPLE CORER: used for removing the apple core and pips without cutting the apple.

COLANDER: used for draining and straining foods.

CONICAL STRAINER: used for straining liquids, custards, gravies, sauces.

CUTTING BOARD: used for cutting fruit, vegetables, fish and meat.

DRAINING LADLE: used for removing pieces of food from a liquid.

EGG LIFTER: used for lifting fried eggs, fish, fritters and other food from frying pan.

GARLIC PRESS: used for crushing garlic.

GRATER: used for shredding or grating foods such as carrots, cabbage or cheese.

ICE CREAM SCOOP: used for ice cream, helps to control the size of each ice cream portion.

KITCHEN SHEARS: used for cutting paper, parsley etc.

LEMON SQUEEZER: used for squeezing oranges or lemons.

MELON BALLER: used for making melon or watermelon balls, also used for making butter balls.

METAL TONGS: used for turning meat and fried food during cooking, and also for serving food like meat, chicken pieces and baked potatoes.

MORTAR AND PESTLE: used for grinding spices.

PASTRY BLENDER: used for blending shortening with flour, making scones, pastry, crushing berries.

PEELER: used for removing fruit and vegetable peels and for making garnishes.

POTATO MASHER: used for mashing potatoes or flattening refrigerator biscuits.

POTATO PRESS: used for making lump-free mashed potato.

SKEWERS: used for testing baked products, and also for threading sosaties or kebabs.

SOUP LADLE: used for basting, and serving liquid foods.

SPATULA: used for turning meat, patties and smaller meat cuts, and for shaping patties and croquettes.

WOODEN MALLET: used for softening meat fibres.

WOODEN SPOON: used for stirring and mixing; wooden spoons absorb grease and odours.

CROCKERY
Dessert bowls
Glasses and water jugs
Glass platters
Mixing bowls
Oven-proof casserole dishes
Salad bowls and servers
Shallow pie dish
Tea and dinner service

FRYING PANS
Cast iron crêpe pan
18 cm pan
25 cm with lid
Roasting pan

CUTLERY
Bread knife with serrated edge
Canteen of dining cutlery
Carving knife and fork
18–20 cm cook's knife
15 cm paring knife with serrated edge
Cutlery and plate drainer
Measuring spoons and cups
Slotted spoon
Soup ladle
Variety of stainless steel serving spoons
Wooden spoons in various sizes

SAUCEPANS
18 cm with lid
23 cm with lid
3,5 litre soup pot

STORAGE
Cake and biscuit tins
Canisters
Plastic storage containers
Storage bins

BAKING UTENSILS

BALLOON WHISK: used only for whipping foods in order to incorporate air.

BEATER, ELECTRIC: used for beating air into a mixture.

BEATER, ROTARY: used for whisk air into foods, blending foods.

DOUGHNUT CUTTER: used for cutting doughnuts.

FLAN RINGS: for making flans.

FLAT BAKING SHEETS: used for scones and other pastries.

FLOUR DREDGER: used for sifting a thin layer of flour where dough is manipulated or rolled out.

FLUTED CUTTERS: used for cutting sweet confectionery (unfluted cutters are normally used for savoury foods).

ICING UTENSILS: syringe and nozzles are used for applying icing.

LOAF TIN: used for bread, fruit and meat loaves.

MIXING BOWLS: used for creaming butter and sugar; mixing dry and liquid ingredients.

MUFFIN PAN: used for muffins.

NYLON PIPING BAGS: used for meringue tubes for shaping biscuits, and piping potatoes.

OVEN-PROOF SCALLOP SHELL: used for seafood au gratin.

PASTRY BOARD: used for rolling pastries and dough out on.

PASTRY BRUSH: used for brushing glaze onto food, and for greasing baking tins.

PASTRY CUTTER: used for mixing shortening and flour when using the cutting-in method.

PASTRY WHEEL: used for cutting lattice strips and trimming edges.

ROLLING PIN: used for rolling out dough or pastries.

ROUND BAKING TIN: used for large cakes.

SAVARIN MOULD: used for brioches.

SIEVE: used for sifting dry ingredients.

SIFTER: used for sifting small quantities of dry ingredients.

SPATULA: used for scraping left-over mixtures from bowls.

SPRINGFORM TIN WITH TUBE: used for cakes and moulds.

SQUARE PAN: used for biscuits that are to be cut up into fingers or squares.

SWISS ROLL PAN: used for Swiss roll cakes and biscuit squares.

WIRE COOLING RACKS: used for cooling cakes and biscuits.

STORE CUPBOARD ESSENTIALS

The following commodities, stored at room temperature, are useful to have on hand.

baking powder	cream of tartar	jam	oil, olive and	sauces, bottled
bicarbonate of soda	curry powder	jelly powder	sunflower	soups, canned
breakfast cereal	custard powder	lemon juice	Orley Whip (long–life	soups, packets
canned fish	dried fruit	lentils	cream)	spices
canned fruit	dried herbs	long-life milk, custard	pasta	sugar, brown
canned vegetables	eggs	and yoghurt	peanut butter	sugar, white
castor sugar	essences	marinades	pickles	Tastee wheat
cherries	evaporated milk	mealie meal	pulses	tea
chillies	garlic paste	milk powder	rice	tomato paste
cocoa	ginger paste	milk shake powder	rose water and syrup	vinegar
coffee	gelatine	mustard (powder	sago, tapioca,	Worcestershire sauce
condensed milk	ground spices	and prepared)	semolina	flour – cake, bread,
cooking chocolate	honey	nuts	salad dressing, bottled	self-raising, whole–
cornflour	icing sugar	oats (quick–cooking)	salt and pepper	wheat

Appetising Snacks and Starters

An elaborate and edible work of art,
a magnificent array of colours, rich
in taste. Scrumptious in the use of
vegetables, nuts and seeds.
Elegantly presented with a variety of
tantalising flavours.

PECAN AND SUNDRIED TOMATO TARTLETS
A tartlet with a complete difference

Cheese pastry
- 150 g cake flour
- 2 ml salt
- 2 ml paprika
- 3 ml baking powder
- 50 g butter
- 50 g finely grated cheddar cheese
- 1 egg yolk
- 60 ml iced water

Filling
- 2 medium onions, finely chopped
- 60 ml oil
- 10 ml garlic, finely crushed
- 100 g pecan nuts, roughly chopped
- 30 ml chutney of choice
- 100 ml sundried tomatoes, finely chopped
- 10 ml paprika
- salt to taste

To make the pastry, sift the dry ingredients into a bowl. Rub in butter. Mix in grated cheese.

Combine egg yolk and water and cut into dry ingredients until the mixture binds. Do not over–mix. Shape dough into a neat square and chill, covered, for 30 minutes.

Cut dough into 5 or 6 pieces. Roll out 1 piece at a time into a long narrow strip the width of the pastry cutter (about 5 cm). Cut 5-cm rounds and press into 4.5-cm mini-muffin pans. Prick well. Layer inside with a piece of prepared greaseproof paper and place 4–6 dried beans in each.

Bake at 180 °C for about 15 minutes, until lightly browned. Remove beans and allow to cool.

To make the filling, sauté the onions in the oil very slowly, adding water and cooking until soft and golden. Add garlic, pecans, chutney, seasonings and sundried tomatoes. Cook for a further 2 minutes.

Just before serving, spoon the filling into the pastry cases. Garnish with dhania.

Makes 24

POTATO WARA
Potato balls enclosed in batter

Batter
- 250 ml pea flour
- 40 ml melted butter or margarine
- salt to taste
- 5 ml garlic paste
- enough water to make a soft dough

oil for deep frying

Filling
- 3 large potatoes, cooked and well mashed
- 10 ml garlic paste
- 2 green chillies, finely chopped
- salt to taste
- 5 ml turmeric
- 5 ml cayenne pepper
- 5 ml whole mustard seeds (optional)
- 50 ml fresh dhania, finely chopped
- cornflour for rolling

Batter
Mix all ingredients together to make a soft batter. Leave aside to settle.

Filling
Add all ingredients to the potatoes, except cornflour, and mix well.

Make ping pong–sized balls with filling and roll each ball in cornflour.

Meanwhile, heat oil till moderately hot. Dip balls into batter, taking care that batter covers the balls completely, and fry till golden brown. Drain.

Serve as a vegetarian dish, accompanied by a chilli sauce.

Makes 20–24

Pecan and sundried tomato tartlets

TUNA SAVOURY PUFFS
Awakens the appetite

Pastry
- 250 ml water
- 100 g margarine or butter
- 5 ml salt
- 10 ml garlic paste
- 250 ml cake flour (sift flour twice in separate bowl)
- 3 eggs at room temperature
- sesame seeds or poppy seeds for sprinkling

Filling
- 2 tins tuna chunks, drained
- 1 medium onion, finely chopped
- 2 green chillies, chopped
- 60 ml chopped dhania leaves
- 5 ml salt

Preheat oven to 200 °C. Place water, butter, salt and garlic into a pot and bring to the boil.

Add flour all at once, stirring vigorously until mixture leaves the sides of the pot clean. Remove from heat and leave to cool.

Beat eggs in one at a time until smooth and well-blended. The mixture should be of a dropping consistency that is soft and glossy, but still holds its shape.

Drop teaspoonfuls of mixture onto a greased baking sheet. Sprinkle with seeds, pressing down lightly for seeds to stick onto pastry.

Bake for 10–15 minutes at 200 °C, then reduce heat to 180 °C and bake until crispy, for about another 10 minutes. Remove from oven.

Slit puffs for steam to escape. Allow to cool.

Make filling by mixing all ingredients together. Pile filling into puffs and arrange on a tray attractively.

Makes 36

CORN AND SPINACH SAVOURY LAGAN
Yellow and green savoury squares

- 200 ml self-raising flour
- 5 ml salt
- 2 ml pepper
- 5 ml turmeric
- 5 ml jeera powder
- 5 ml koljana powder
- 5 ml crushed chillies
- ½ bunch fresh dhania, chopped
- 2 green chillies, chopped
- 410 g can cream-style sweetcorn
- 30 ml soft butter
- 1 bunch spinach, washed and finely shredded
- 2 eggs, beaten

Preheat oven to 180 °C.

Sift all dry ingredients together. Mix in all other ingredients and stir in eggs.

Pour mixture into a well-greased oven-proof dish and bake until set, for about 30 minutes. Cool down and cut into squares.

Serve on a large round platter with a chutney dip. Garnish as desired.

Makes 24–30

Tuna savoury puffs

MUSHROOM PALMIERS
A dainty pastry with layers of mushroom filling

- 500 g puff pastry
- 1 egg, lightly beaten

Filling
- 15 ml oil
- 15 g butter
- 15 ml crushed garlic
- 1 green chilli, finely chopped
- 1 medium onion, finely chopped
- 250 g mushrooms, finely chopped
- 15 ml cake flour
- 30 ml water (if needed)
- 30 ml chopped parsley
- salt to taste
- pepper to taste
- lightly beaten egg
- sesame seeds for sprinkling

Preheat oven to 200 °C.

Heat oil and butter in a saucepan. Add garlic, chilli and onion. Cook, stirring, until onion mixture is soft.

Add mushrooms; cook for 5 minutes or until mushrooms are soft, stirring regularly. Add flour, salt and pepper and stir over heat for a minute.

Gradually stir in water; keep stirring until mixture boils and thickens. Remove from heat and cool. Stir in parsley.

Assembly
Roll out pastry on a lightly floured surface to a 25 cm x 35 cm rectangle. Divide lengths into three without cutting through pastry.

Spread filling over 2 ends leaving the centre unfilled. Roll each filled end like a Swiss roll towards centre, making it stick with beaten egg.

Refrigerate for 30 minutes. Cut roll into 1-cm slices. Place cut side up on sprayed baking sheets. Neaten palmiers and brush with beaten egg. Sprinkle with sesame seeds. Bake for 12–15 minutes until golden. Serve with a tangy dip.

Makes 20

SAVOURY ROULADE
A decadent Swiss roll with a complete difference

- 60 ml margarine or butter
- 2.5 ml crushed garlic
- 1 green chilli, finely chopped
- 10 ml fresh dhania
- 5 ml salt
- 60 g cake flour
- 500 ml milk
- 4 extra-large eggs, separated

Preheat oven to 160 °C.

Melt margarine or butter; add garlic, chilli and dhania. Stir in flour and salt.

Gradually add milk, stirring constantly, to make a smooth sauce. Cool down slightly. Beat in egg yolks. Beat egg whites with a pinch of salt until stiff. Gently fold into batter with a metal spoon.

Line a greased Swiss roll baking tray with baking paper and spray the paper well with non-stick spray. Spread batter evenly in baking tray.

Bake for 45 minutes. Remove from oven. Turn roulade out onto greaseproof paper. Trim edges. Spread filling of choice on roulade and roll up, Swiss-roll style.

Filling
Tuna and mayonnaise; braised chicken; spicy potato.

Makes 1

Variation: For a centrepiece, spread top and sides with cottage cheese and sprinkle with black poppy seeds, or alternate with rows of seeds then very finely chopped parsley.

Mushroom palmiers

SPANAKOPITA
Spicy spinach-filled phyllo pastry triangles

Pastry
- 1 box phyllo pastry
- 100g melted butter

Filling
- 1 bunch spinach, washed, chopped, steamed and squeezed dry
- 30ml cooking oil
- 1 medium onion, finely chopped
- 10ml crushed garlic
- 10ml peri-peri powder
- 5ml paprika
- pinch of nutmeg
- 5ml pepper
- 100ml fresh parsley, finely chopped
- 250g crumbled cottage or feta cheese
- salt and black pepper to taste

Sauté onion with garlic in oil and combine all filling ingredients, mixing well. Keep aside.

Work on greaseproof paper. Place one sheet of phyllo on paper and brush with melted butter. Cover with a second piece of pastry and brush with melted butter. Cut into 8-cm wide continuous strips, using a pastry wheel or a sharp knife.

Place a teaspoon of filling at the base of each strip and fold into triangle. Continue until all pastry and filling is used up.

Brush with butter and bake on a greased baking tray at 200°C for 15-20 minutes or until lightly golden.

Allow to cool before serving.

Makes 36-40

Note: While working with phyllo pastry, cover the sheets not being used with a damp cloth to prevent drying out.

CHEESY CHILLI SESAME BALLS
A crispy cocktail biscuit with golden sesame seeds

- 310 ml cake flour
- 2 ml cayenne pepper
- 125 g butter, chopped
- 40 g cream cheese
- 375 ml grated cheddar cheese
- 15 ml chopped fresh dhania or parsley
- 80 ml sesame seeds

Preheat oven to 180 °C. Prepare a 32 cm x 28 cm biscuit tray.

Place flour and cayenne pepper in a food processor.

Add butter, cheese and dhania. Using the pulse action, work butter for 15–20 seconds or until mixture almost forms a soft dough. Do not over–beat.

Turn mixture into a large mixing bowl. Press together with fingers to form a soft dough.

Roll two level teaspoons of mixture into a ball. Roll ball in sesame seeds. Repeat until all dough is used up.

Arrange balls on prepared tray about 3 cm apart.

Bake for 20–25 minutes, or until golden. Remove from oven. Allow to cool for 5 minutes, then remove to wire rack to cool completely.

Makes 25–30

TULIP BASKETS FILLED WITH COTTAGE CHEESE AND SALMON

- 1 box phyllo pastry
- 100 g melted butter

Filling
- 250 g mascarpone cheese
- 45 ml fat–free plain yoghurt
- 300 g smoked salmon
- chives or herbs for garnishing

Preheat oven to 180 °C.

Use pastry as per instructions on the box. Cut into 7 cm x 7 cm squares using 4 squares and brushing each layer with butter.

Layer each square to form a 12–pointed star. Press squares lightly to form a tulip basket.

Bake for 12–15 minutes till golden brown. Remove from oven and allow to cool.

Mix cream cheese with plain yoghurt; pipe into baskets.Place salmon decoratively on the cheese mixture.

Garnish with chives.

Makes 40

TULIP BASKETS FILLED WITH CHICKEN AND SUNDRIED TOMATO

- 1 box phyllo pastry
- 100 g melted butter

Filling
- 2 medium onions, finely chopped
- 60 ml oil
- 2 chicken breasts, cubed
- 10 ml garlic, finely crushed
- 100 g pecan nuts, roughly chopped
- 30 ml chutney of choice
- 100 ml sundried tomatoes, chopped into small pieces
- 10 ml paprika
- salt to taste

Preheat oven to 180 °C.

Use pastry as per instructions on the box. Cut phyllo into 7 cm x 7 cm squares using 4 squares and brushing each layer with butter.

Layer each square to form a 12–pointed star. Press squares lightly to form a tulip basket.

Bake for 12–15 minutes till golden brown.

Allow to cool.

Filling
Sauté the onions in oil until soft and golden. Add chicken and cook for a further 5–7 minutes. Add garlic, pecans, chutney, seasonings and chopped sundried tomatoes. Cook for a further 2 minutes.

Just before serving, spoon the filling into the pastry cases. Garnish with dhania.

Makes 40

Tulip baskets

FILLED SPINACH PANCAKES
Simply divine and cheesy

- 250 ml finely shredded spinach, washed and drained
- 325 ml milk
- 15 ml margarine or butter, melted
- 2 eggs
- 250 ml cake flour (use a little more if required)
- 5 ml baking powder
- 5 ml fine jeera powder
- 5 ml turmeric
- 2 green chillies, finely chopped
- 1 medium onion, finely chopped
- salt to taste

Filling
- 250 ml smooth cottage cheese
- 100 ml grated cheese

Liquidise the spinach with some of the milk. Beat the rest of the milk with the margarine or butter and eggs until frothy. Sift dry ingredients into the milk mixture and beat until smooth.

Add spinach, chillies and onion to the batter. Mix well and adjust seasoning. Batter must be smooth and spreadable. Rest for 10–15 minutes.

Heat a non–stick frying pan and grease well with non–stick cooking spray. Pour a thin layer of batter evenly into the pan and fry to a delicate colour on both sides. Spread with cottage cheese mixture. Roll up like a Swiss roll.

Serve with sweet and sour sauce, or soy sauce on the side.

Makes 12–15

MINI–PIES WITH SOUR CREAM PASTRY
A soft delicious pastry, slightly layered

- 750 ml cake flour
- 2 ml salt
- 250 g butter, cut into small blocks
- 250 ml smetana or cultured sour cream

Mince filling
- 400 g mince
- 1 medium onion, finely chopped
- oil
- 5 ml salt
- 5 ml jeera powder
- 5 ml cayenne pepper
- 3 ml turmeric
- 5 ml koljana powder
- 10 ml garlic and ginger paste
- 50 ml dhania, finely chopped

Preheat oven to 200 °C. Grease 2 baking trays; keep them to one side.

Sift flour and salt twice. Rub butter into the flour mixture until it resembles breadcrumbs. Pour all the sour cream into the flour mixture at once and mix into a firm dough.

Use your hands to bind the pastry. Do not add water. Bring together and cover with plastic. Leave to rest in the fridge for 30 minutes. Roll and fold three times. Allow the pastry to rest. Roll and fold twice more, and use as required.

Filling
Rinse and drain mince in colander. (Never leave the mince in water as it will be waterlogged.)

In a pot, braise the onion in a little oil till golden. Add mince and mix well. Add spices, garlic and ginger and blend well. Braise mince till done and fairly dry. Add dhania and mix well.

Assembly
Use a flower cutter to cut pastry into rounds. Fill each round with filling and cover with another round of pastry as for pies. Brush with egg and sprinkle with poppy seeds.

Bake at 200 °C for 15 minutes and then at 180 °C until golden.

Makes 15–20

Note: This pastry improves with standing and can be made 3–4 days in advance. It may also be frozen for up to 6 months.

MINI PITAS
Crispy, flavoursome and succulent

- 500 g cake flour
- 5 ml salt
- 5 ml sugar
- 1 packet instant dry yeast
- 1 egg
- 60 ml oil
- 180 ml lukewarm water (approximate)

Filling
- 30 ml oil
- 1 onion, chopped
- 500 g chicken mince
- 15 ml paprika
- 15 ml Cajun spice
- 15 ml barbeque spice
- 10 ml garlic and ginger paste
- 100 ml mayonnaise
- salt to taste

Preheat oven to 180 °C. Spray a baking tray with non-stick cooking spray.

Sift flour, salt and sugar together. Sprinkle with yeast and mix through. Beat together egg and oil; add water and mix. Add to dry ingredients. Mix into a soft dough, adding more water if necessary.

On a table, knead dough until it is smooth and elastic. Lightly oil a clean bowl and place dough in it. Lightly smear the top of the dough with oil and cover with cling wrap. Place bowl in a warm place and allow dough to double in size – about 45 minutes. Once risen, knock down.

Divide dough in half. Take one half and roll into a sausage. Cut into small pieces and roll each piece into a smooth ball. Ball must be about the size of a walnut. Allow balls to double in size.

On a lightly floured surface, flatten balls and, with a round cutter, cut into even-sized rounds. Bake for about 5–7 minutes until baked through. Do not over-bake or they will be too brown and dry; a pita bread tends to be light in colour. Remove to cooling rack and cover with a damp cloth to keep soft.

Make filling. Heat oil in a large pan. Add onion and fry until soft and transparent. Add spices and chicken and stir-fry for 8–10 minutes.

Cool chicken mixture and stir in mayonnaise.

When ready to serve, cut pitas in half, but not entirely through. Pile chicken stir-fry into the pita pockets and serve immediately.

Makes 36

Note: Whilst shaping each pita, place on baking tray and cover the pitas with a damp cloth to prevent them from rising too much. A tray of water may be placed at the bottom of the oven to create steam. This keeps the pitas soft.

Mini pitas

GARLIC STEAK FOLD–OVERS
Golden yellow, crisp fried pastry puff with a steak filling

Pastry
- 500 ml cake flour
- 10 ml baking powder
- 5 ml garlic salt
- 60 ml melted butter
- 100 ml warm milk (use enough to make a soft dough)
- 2 ml yellow food colouring

Steak filling
- 40 g margarine or butter
- 500 g steak, cut into thin fine strips
- 15 ml garlic paste
- 5 ml koljana powder
- 10 ml barbeque spice
- 5 ml paprika
- 2 ml black pepper
- 5 ml fine mustard powder
- egg white
- salt to taste
- oil for deep frying

Pastry
Sift all dry ingredients twice into a bowl. Blend milk, butter and food colouring well. Add to flour and form a soft dough. Use more milk if required. Knead dough on a smooth surface until glossy. Place in a greased bowl and allow to rest for 15–20 minutes. Meanwhile, prepare filling.

Filling
Melt margarine or butter. Add washed and drained meat and braise in pot for 5 minutes, tossing all the time. Add a little water and cook for 2–5 minutes. Add all spices and cook till done and meat is soft. Leave to cool.

Assembly
Roll pastry into a large sausage. Cut sausage into 3 pieces. Roll into round balls and allow to rest. Roll each ball into a circle and cut into rounds with the desired cookie cutter size.

Place filling on one half. Brush edges with beaten egg white.

Fold the other half of pastry over and seal well. Place on greaseproof paper that has been sprayed with non–stick cooking spray. Continue with the rest of pastry and filling. Cover with a damp cloth.

Frying
Use enough oil to deep–fry. Fry pastries a few at a time in moderately heated oil over medium heat. Spoon oil over pastry to create a puff when frying. Drain.

Serve hot with a tasty dip.

Makes 36–40

BAKED CHICKEN SAVOURY ROUNDS
'Chicken Lagan' with a difference

- 500 g chicken mince
- 10 ml ginger and garlic paste
- 25 ml ground almonds
- 25 ml butter or margarine
- 2 green chillies, chopped finely
- 2.5 ml pepper
- 5 ml jeera powder
- 5 ml salt
- 1 bunch dhania leaves
- 3 slices white bread
- 180 ml milk
- 10 ml baking powder
- 5 eggs, separated
- sesame seeds for sprinkling

Preheat oven to 180 °C. Prepare 2 muffin trays.

Mix together first 8 ingredients. Place in a pot and braise till nearly dry, but not browned. Cool mixture and set aside.

Blend dhania, bread, milk, baking powder and egg yolks in liquidiser. Pour into a bowl, add chicken mixture as well.

In a separate bowl, beat egg whites until stiff. Fold into chicken with a metal spoon.

Pour mixture into greased muffin pans. Bake at 180 °C for 30 minutes. Halfway through baking time, sprinkle top with sesame seeds. Continue baking till done. Do not brown.

Serve with a green salad.

Makes 30–36

SAVOURY CHEESE BAKLAVA
These mouth-watering cheese and onion diamonds are best eaten warm

- 100 g butter or margarine, melted
- 1 box phyllo pastry

Filling
- 30 g butter or margarine
- 2 medium onions, chopped finely
- 30 ml garlic paste
- 10 ml cayenne pepper
- 30 ml sesame seeds
- 30 ml poppy seeds
- 10 ml lemon pepper
- 300 g feta cheese, crumbled
- 225 g chunky cottage cheese
- 500 g grated sweetmilk cheese
- 2 eggs, beaten
- 30 ml milk
- salt to taste

Topping
- 50 ml walnuts, finely chopped
- paprika powder for sprinkling
- honey for drizzling

Melt butter or margarine. Add onions and sauté until golden brown. Add a little water if necessary.

Add garlic and sauté for a further 2 minutes, stirring all the time. Place onions in bowl. Add spices, seeds and cheeses and blend well. Add beaten eggs and blend well.

Add milk and mix through. In separate bowls, divide filling into 3 and keep aside.

Assembly
Preheat oven to 200 °C. Use an oven tray of a large enough size to accommodate the phyllo sheets; spray with non-stick cooking spray.

Unwrap phyllo pastry and cover with damp cloth to prevent drying out. Lay 2 sheets of pastry in baking tray and brush with melted butter. Lay 2 more sheets on top and brush with butter.

Layer with first bowl of cheese filling. Layer with 2 sheets of phyllo. Brush with butter. Repeat this twice more.

Layer evenly with the second bowl of filling. Cover with 2 sheets of pastry and brush with butter. Repeat twice more.

Layer with the third bowl of filling. Continue layering with phyllo in sets of 2 until all pastry is used. Brush top liberally with butter and cut into diamond-shaped pieces.

Bake for 15 minutes and top with honey, walnuts and paprika.

Makes 24-30

Savoury cheese baklava

CREAMY CHICKEN HORNS
A creamy tantalising savoury

Filling
- 500 g chicken fillets, cut into small pieces
- 5 ml salt
- 5 ml peri-peri
- 5 ml chicken spice
- 30 ml oil
- 125 ml mayonnaise
- 30 ml sweet chilli sauce

Pastry horns
- 500 g puff pastry
- 1 egg, beaten
- poppy seeds for garnish
- rosemary sprigs for garnish
- cherry tomatoes for garnish, cut into slices

Preheat oven to 200 °C. Spray a baking sheet with non-stick cooking spray.

Make the filling first. Wash and drain chicken. Sprinkle with salt and spices. Heat oil in a pot and add chicken. Stir-fry until chicken is cooked. Allow to cool thoroughly.

Mix mayonnaise and chilli sauce together; fold in chicken and mix well.

Pastry horns
Spray pastry horn moulds with non-stick cooking spray. Roll out pastry to a thickness of 3 mm. Cut into 1.5 cm strips.

Wind each strip of pastry around mould, allowing it to overlap. Use only half the horn since cocktail or dainty mini-horns are more pleasing.

Brush tops with beaten egg and sprinkle poppy seeds. Place on baking sheet and bake until golden.

Remove pastry from moulds and allow to cool thoroughly. Fill pastry horns with filling and garnish with a sprig of rosemary and a slice of cherry tomato.

Makes 15–20

Variation: Add chopped peppers, spring onions and diced cucumber to chicken filling. Tuna, mince or steak may also be used to fill the horns.

Creamy chicken horns

CHAPTER TWO

Nutritious Soups

Treat your family with warm, bold
nutritious innovation. Soups remain the
most wholesome and traditional of liquid
foods, even though they have been
reinvented over the centuries. Good,
simple and hearty goodness.

CREAMY MUSHROOM SOUP
A mouth-watering, creamy soup

- 1 medium onion, chopped
- 1 punnet fresh mushrooms, chopped
- 15 ml butter
- 1 can mushroom soup
- 2 cans water
- 1 packet mushroom soup
- 250 ml milk
- salt
- black pepper
- 125 ml cream
- 15 ml chives, chopped for garnish

Sauté onion and mushrooms gently in butter. Add the can of mushroom soup and 2 cans of water. Boil for 10 minutes.

Add packet of soup made into a thin paste, as per instructions on packet.

Add milk and boil for 15 minutes. Season with salt and pepper. Add the fresh cream and blend well.

Leave to stand for 5 minutes and garnish with chives. Serve with crusty brown bread.

Serves 4–6

CHICKEN AND CORN SOUP
A deliciously divine creamy taste

- 10 ml butter or margarine
- 2 onions, finely chopped
- 250 g chicken breasts, cubed
- 410 g can cream-style sweetcorn
- 750 ml milk
- 500 ml water
- 10 ml chicken spice
- 10 ml white pepper
- 5 ml salt
- 30 ml cornflour
- 1 celery stick, chopped
- 200 g fresh cream

In a large pot over medium heat, sauté butter or margarine; add onions and braise well.

Add chicken to onions and stir-fry over moderate heat for 7 minutes.

Add sweetcorn, milk, water, spice and seasoning. Combine cornflour with a little water to make a thin paste. Pour into soup and stir until it has thickened.

Add chopped celery and bring to a fast boil for 5 minutes. Remove from heat and stir in fresh cream. Serve immediately.

Serves 4–6

Creamy mushroom soup

POTATO AND LEEK SOUP
Delectable, silky smooth and creamy

- 15 ml cooking oil
- 1 medium onion, chopped
- 500 g potatoes, peeled and diced
- 500 g trimmed leeks, sliced
- 500 ml milk
- 500 ml water
- 150 ml cream
- 2 ml nutmeg
- 10 ml salt
- 10 ml white pepper
- chopped parsley for garnish

Warm oil in a large saucepan over moderate heat. Add onion. Cover and cook for 5 minutes.

Add potatoes and leeks. Stir well and cook for 10 minutes.

Pour in milk and water; bring to the boil for 5 minutes, stirring, then simmer until vegetables are tender.

Allow to cool slightly. Liquidise until smooth. Return to pot and stir in cream and seasonings.

Reheat gently and garnish with parsley. Serve with home–baked bread.

Serves 4–6

MINESTRONE SOUP
A wonderful soup using vegetables you have in your kitchen

- 15 ml butter
- 15 ml oil
- 1 large onion, finely chopped
- 1 leek, finely chopped
- 2 sticks celery, diced
- 2 large carrots, diced
- 2 tomatoes, chopped
- 1 clove garlic, crushed
- ¼ cabbage, finely shredded
- 1 can tomato soup mixed with 1 litre water
- 1 can haricot beans
- 4 peppercorns
- 4 cloves
- 50 g spaghetti (optional)
- 5 ml salt
- 10 ml white pepper

In a large saucepan, heat together the butter and oil. Add all vegetables and garlic.

Fry gently for 10 minutes, covered, stirring occasionally to prevent vegetables from sticking.

Pour in the water mixed with tomato soup; add beans and spices. Boil for 10 minutes.

Add spaghetti and cook for a further 30 minutes.

Adjust seasoning if necessary. Serve with crusty bread.

Serves 4–6

Minestrone soup

CREAM OF CARROT SOUP
Flavoursome and refreshing

- 50 g butter
- 1 bunch carrots, peeled and sliced
- 2 medium onions, chopped finely
- 30 ml crushed garlic
- 3 medium potatoes, diced
- 500 ml water
- 10 ml salt
- 5 ml cayenne pepper
- 5 ml white pepper
- 500 ml milk
- 250 ml fresh cream

In a large saucepan, melt butter. Add carrots, onions and garlic. Cook over low heat for 5 minutes, stirring from time to time to prevent vegetables from sticking.

Add potatoes, water and seasonings. Simmer for 20 minutes, or until vegetables are tender. Remove from heat and allow to cool slightly before liquidising.

Return to clean pot and reheat gently. Add milk and bring to the boil. Adjust seasoning.

Pour cream into soup just before serving, keeping a little aside for decoration. Blend well.

Swirl with remaining cream and garnish as desired. Serve with crusty bread.

Serves 4–6

CREAMY BUTTERNUT SOUP
Simply a 'must have' recipe

- 25 ml oil
- 10 ml butter
- 1 large onion, chopped
- 500 g butternut, cubed
- 1 medium potato, peeled and cubed
- 5 ml turmeric
- 5 ml curry powder
- 2 ml ground cinnamon
- 500 ml water
- 5 ml salt
- 5 ml sugar
- 500 ml milk
- 250 ml fresh cream
- chopped chives for garnishing

Heat oil and butter in a large saucepan. Add onion and sauté until golden.

Add butternut, potato and spices. Toss together over low heat for 2 minutes until well-coated.

Add water, salt and sugar. Bring to the boil, then cover and simmer gently until vegetables are soft; about 25 minutes. Cool.

Purée mixture in a blender until smooth. Return mixture to saucepan and reheat, adding milk and cream to achieve a medium–thick consistency.

Garnish with chopped chives.

Serves 4–6

Cream of carrot soup

CHAPTER THREE
3

Tantalising Salads and Wholesome Vegetables

It's amazing how a simple combination of fresh salad ingredients can transform an ordinary mélange of lettuce leaves into a tasty sensation. Salads need not merely be an accompaniment. They make wonderful main meals. Open a treasure trove of ideas for new ways to combine the freshest seasonal bounty. Get inspired by the fresh healthy appeal of vegetables, be it cooked or raw. They are the tastiest and healthiest foods. Be spontaneous with flavours and further enhance the robust goodness of vegetables.

CHUNKY VEGETABLE CURRY
A tasty, versatile curry

- 60 ml oil
- 1 medium onion, sliced finely
- 30 ml garlic and ginger paste
- 10 ml cayenne pepper
- 5 ml turmeric
- 5 ml barishap powder
- 10 ml koljana powder
- 5 ml jeera powder
- 5 ml whole mustard seeds
- 2 tomatoes, finely chopped
- 5 medium carrots, cut into chunks
- 3 medium potatoes, cubed
- 250 g cauliflower, broken into florets
- 125 g green beans, cut into 5–cm pieces
- 100 g mushrooms, sliced or whole
- 100 g green peas
- 100 g baby corn
- 20 ml chopped fresh dhania
- salt to taste

Heat oil in a large pot. Add onion and cook till soft and transparent.

Add spices and tomatoes. Add a little water to make a thick sauce. Add potatoes and carrots and simmer till half–done.

Add cauliflower, beans and a little water if necessary. Simmer for 5 minutes.

Add all other ingredients and simmer till vegetables are tender yet retain their crispness.

Sprinkle with dhania and serve with white rice, either as a main course or as a side dish.

Serves 6–8

GRILLED PINEAPPLE INDULGENCE
An unusual, delicious starter

- 1 large pineapple, cut into thick slices
- 100 ml brown sugar
- 30 ml butter
- 15 ml oil
- 150 ml honey, warmed
- 2 red chillies, thinly sliced
- 2 green chillies, thinly sliced
- 15 ml paprika
- dhania leaves for garnishing

Sprinkle the pineapple with the brown sugar on both sides.

Heat a griddle pan and place pineapple rings on the hot griddle for 2–3 minutes on each side, or until golden brown in colour (the pineapple must still be slightly crunchy).

Remove from pan and place pineapple slices loosely on top of one another.

Pour the honey over the pineapple tower; dust with paprika. Sprinkle the sliced chillies on and around the pineapple and garnish with fresh coriander leaves.

Serve immediately as a starter to whet the appetite.

Serves 6–8

Chunky vegetable curry

HERBED STIR-FRIED VEGGIE PASTA SALAD
Serve as a main course, crunchy and tangy

- 200 g bowtie pasta
- 1 red pepper, cut in half and pips removed
- 1 yellow pepper, cut in half and pips removed
- 6–8 carrots
- 1 punnet mushrooms
- 6–8 baby marrows, washed
- 100 g snow peas
- 100 g walnuts, halved (optional)
- 100 g sundried tomatoes, cut into strips
- oil for stir-frying
- salt to taste

Dressing
- 125 ml oil
- 60 ml lemon juice
- 5 ml dried mixed herbs
- 20 ml crushed garlic
- 2 chillies, finely chopped
- salt to taste

Prepare the dressing first by whisking all ingredients together. Check seasoning and adjust to personal taste. Leave aside until required.

Preheat oven to 180 °C.

Cook pasta in lots of boiling water until *al dente*. Rinse well, and drain. Once cooled, place pasta in a large bowl and keep aside.

Rub the skin of the red and yellow pepper with a little oil and roast at 180 °C until skin blisters. Remove from oven and place in a plastic bag to sweat. Once cooled, peel the skin off the peppers. Slice peppers into neat strips and keep aside.

Cut carrots into julienne strips and keep aside. Slice mushrooms and keep aside. Cut the baby marrows in half lengthwise and then cut each half at an angle forming half moons.

Heat a wok or fairly large pan. Add a little oil and stir-fry carrots until just soft, they must still retain their shape and colour. Add to pasta and mix.

Stir-fry mushrooms until just browned. Add to pasta and mix. Stir-fry marrows until just soft. Add to pasta and mix. Season with salt.

Mix in the sliced peppers, sundried tomatoes and nuts. Pour the dressing over the warm veggies and pasta and mix through gently.

Place in a decorative bowl and serve at room temperature.

Serves 8–10

Herbed stir–fried veggie pasta salad

CREAMY NOODLE AND CORN SALAD
Refreshingly appetising

- 1 English cucumber, diced
- 1 green pepper, diced
- 1 red pepper, diced
- 1 medium onion, finely chopped
- 15 ml crushed garlic
- ½ bunch parsley, finely chopped
- 1 can corn kernels, drained
- 500 ml screw noodles, cooked
- 5 ml white pepper
- 250 ml mayonnaise
- salt to taste

Toss all ingredients together and mix well with the mayonnaise. Season to taste.

Serve as a main meal or as an accompaniment to a roast.

Serves 6–8

LEBANESE BUTTER BEAN SALAD
Delicious as a first course

- 60 ml olive or sunflower oil
- 30 ml garlic paste
- 2 medium onions, thinly sliced
- 1 red pepper, seeded and diced
- 1 green pepper, seeded and diced
- 15 ml mixed herbs
- 30 ml chopped parsley
- 2 cans butter beans, drained and rinsed
- 45 ml fresh lemon juice
- 4 hard–boiled eggs, roughly chopped
- 15 ml paprika
- 45 ml fresh dhania leaves, chopped
- salt and pepper to taste

Heat oil and sauté garlic and onions over medium heat until lightly golden. Add peppers and herbs. Toss well.

Remove from heat and spoon into a bowl. Add all other ingredients, except eggs. Toss lightly. Take care not to make the beans mushy.

Place in a serving bowl. Garnish with boiled eggs and sprinkle with paprika and fresh dhania leaves.

Serve with garlic bread.

Serves 4–6

NUTTY CABBAGE SLAW WITH PINEAPPLE
A delicately–flavoured, delicious crunchy–textured family favourite

- ½ (small) white cabbage, shredded
- ½ (small) red cabbage, shredded
- 3 apples of choice, cut into chunks
- 250 ml seedless raisins
- 1 pineapple, cut into chunks
- 30 ml roasted sesame seeds
- 60 ml flaked almonds
- juice of 2 lemons
- salt to taste

Dressing
- 80 ml olive or cooking oil
- 30 ml white vinegar
- 30 ml honey
- 30 ml crushed garlic
- 60 ml chopped parsley or dhania
- 2 green chillies, finely chopped
- salt and pepper to taste

Place finely shredded cabbage into a large bowl.
  Toss apples with lemon juice.
  Add all salad ingredients together and keep aside.
  Mix dressing ingredients together in a jar and shake well. Sprinkle over salad in bowl.
  Chill and serve as desired.

Serves 6–8

CRUNCHY MEDITERRANEAN SPROUT SALAD
Crunchy and fresh

- 1 pillow–pack assorted leaves
- ½ Chinese cabbage, shredded
- 1 green pepper, sliced
- 1 bunch celery sticks, sliced
- 1 medium onion, thinly sliced
- ½ bunch fresh dhania, chopped
- 3 green chillies, finely chopped
- 100 g baby corn
- 2 carrots, cut into julienne strips
- 100 g mushrooms, sliced
- ½ cucumber, sliced
- 2 tomatoes, cut into quarters
- 50 ml lettuce leaves
- 1 pineapple, cut into chunks
- 100 g walnuts or pine nuts
- salt to taste

Dressing
- 60 ml lemon juice
- 5 ml cooking oil
- 5 ml black pepper
- 15 ml crushed garlic
- 15 ml honey
- 60 ml sesame seeds
- juice of 1 orange

Topping
- 2 feta rounds
- 50 g sprouts

Arrange assorted leaves on a large platter.
  Toss all other salad ingredients together in a large bowl. Mix the salad dressing ingredients together well in a bottle or blender. Pour dressing over salad and toss well. Place the salad on the leaves, and top with feta and sprouts. Serve as required.

Serves 6–8

HOT VEGETABLE SALAD
Crunchy, garlic-flavoured vegetables

- 1 large butternut
- 2 medium red onions, peeled
- 3 large thin, long sweet potatoes
- 12 baby carrots
- 10 whole garlic cloves
- 5 ml dried oregano
- 15 ml paprika
- 10 ml crushed peppercorns
- 5 ml whole cumin
- 5 ml crushed chillies
- 60 ml olive oil
- fresh oregano for garnishing

Preheat oven to 180 °C.

Cut butternut into large chunks; cut red onions into quarters. Cut sweet potato into thick rings and top the carrots. Crush garlic cloves slightly to release their flavour. Toss all vegetables in spices and oil.

Place in a roasting pan; cover with foil and bake for 30–40 minutes. Remove the foil about 15 minutes before vegetables are cooked, to brown slightly. The vegetables must still be crispy.

Garnish with fresh oregano. Serve with roast meats.

Serves 4–6

Note: It is not necessary to peel the vegetables.

TANGY FRUIT AND VEGETABLE SALAD
Divine!

- 1 large onion, sliced
- 10 ml salt
- 60 ml white vinegar
- 30 ml sugar
- 2 red apples, sliced
- 2 green apples, sliced
- 6 celery sticks, sliced
- 2 pineapples, cubed
- 1 green chilli, finely chopped
- 100 ml finely chopped fresh dhania
- 5 ml cayenne pepper

In a bowl, combine onion and salt. Set aside for 10 minutes.

Knead onion slices gently with fingers to soften. Rinse and drain. Pour vinegar and sugar over onion. Set aside.

Combine all salad ingredients with the onion, and sprinkle with cayenne pepper and chill.

Serve with main meal of choice.

Serves 6–8

Hot vegetable salad

AVOCADO MEDLEY
Mouth-wateringly delightful

- 2 medium avocados
- 30 ml lemon juice
- 2 medium tomatoes
- 2 medium potatoes, peeled and cubed
- 30 ml oil
- 1 medium onion, sliced
- 410 g can red kidney beans, drained
- 30 ml cayenne pepper
- 5 ml salt
- 2 ml white pepper
- 15 ml garlic paste
- 30 ml dhania leaves, chopped
- 5 ml Tabasco
- fresh dhania leaves for garnish

Peel and cube avocados. Toss cubes in the lemon juice to prevent discolouration.

Place tomatoes in boiling water for 1 minute; drain, allow to cool. Peel the skin from the tomatoes and cut into cubes. Keep aside.

Parboil the cubed potatoes (the potatoes must be soft, but still hold their shape).

In a medium saucepan, heat oil and sauté onion for 3–5 minutes or until soft. Add potatoes, beans, spices, garlic, dhania and Tabasco. Sauté for a further 5 minutes.

Remove from pan and allow to cool slightly. Place in a bowl and add the tomatoes. Top with avocados and garnish with dhania.

Serve as a starter or with roasts.

Serves 4–6

POTATO AND MAYO SALAD

- 1 kg potatoes, cut into cubes
- 2 medium onions
- 1 green chilli
- 30 ml sunflower oil
- 30 ml white vinegar
- 15 ml mustard powder
- 250 ml mayonnaise
- 1 bunch chopped fresh dhania
- 10 ml peri–peri powder
- 5 ml salt
- 5 ml black pepper

Cook potatoes in boiling salted water until tender. Drain potatoes and dry lightly with absorbent paper.

Chop onions and add the potatoes; leave aside.

Whisk together chilli, oil, vinegar, mustard powder, mayonnaise, dhania, peri–peri, salt and pepper.

Toss and lightly mix into potatoes.

Serve chilled with braised chops or grilled fish.

Serves 4–6

Note: The secret to a good potato salad is to mix the dressing in while the potato is still hot

Avocado medley

WALNUT GREEN SALAD
Crunchy, tangy and fresh

- 1 packet baby spinach or salad leaves
- 1 medium cucumber
- 100 g snow peas
- 4 baby marrows, cut into julienne strips
- 1 green pepper, cut into strips
- 2 green chillies, chopped
- 4 celery sticks, sliced
- 100 g walnuts, halved

Dressing
- 60 ml olive oil
- 30 ml lemon juice
- 30 ml honey
- 10 ml mustard powder
- 5 ml cayenne pepper
- 5 ml white pepper
- 2 ml salt

Place salad leaves in a large flat–bottomed bowl.

Slice cucumber and snow peas and place on top of the leaves.

Layer the rest of the salad ingredients on top of the cucumber and peas.

Pack walnuts in a decorative design on top. Keep salad aside till required.

In a jar, mix dressing ingredients together and shake well. Keep aside.

When ready to serve, drizzle dressing over salad.

Serves 4–6

CHILLI BEAN SALAD
Light, chilli crisp scrumptious salad

- ½ pillow–pack baby spinach leaves
- ½ pillow–pack lettuce leaves
- 1 can red kidney beans
- 1 can chickpeas
- 1 large red pepper, sliced
- 1 large green pepper, sliced
- 1 large yellow pepper, sliced
- 1 papino
- 1 red chilli, chopped finely
- 1 green chilli, chopped finely
- 100 ml slivered almonds
- fresh dhania leaves for garnishing

Dressing
- 30 ml lemon juice
- 100 ml oil
- 5 ml salt
- 5 ml white pepper
- 5 ml garlic paste

Wash and drain lettuce leaves, spinach leaves, red kidney beans and chickpeas.

Make dressing by mixing all ingredients together in a jar and shaking well to combine. Set aside until required.

Peel and slice the papino. Arrange lettuce leaves and spinach leaves on the base of a platter.

Lightly toss remaining ingredients and arrange in the centre of the leaves. Drizzle dressing over the salad.

Enjoy with roast beef.

Serves 4–6

Chilli bean salad

CHAPTER FOUR

Perfect Pasta and Versatile Rice

The secret is in the sauce and there is no denying that it's hard to
beat a delicious bowl of pasta served with your favourite sauce.
Pasta takes many irresistible forms and tastes, with visual variety.
Dishes become 'designer pastas' and contemporary creations
become favourite classics.

Rice is a staple that comes in all shapes, sizes and textures, forming
an authentic accompaniment to many others dishes – rich or simple,
spicy or mild.

Rice is treated with increasing reverence and innovation these
days and is most versatile.

CUBED STEAK WITH CREAMY MUSHROOM AND PENNE
Chunky meat in tasty sauce

Steak
- 1 kg cubed steak
- 30 ml steak and chops spice
- 30 ml paprika
- 30 ml chutney
- 30 ml garlic paste
- 60 ml butter

Pasta
- 300 g penne pasta
- 15 ml cooking oil
- 40 g butter
- 1 medium onion, finely chopped
- 1 punnet mushrooms, sliced
- 1 can mushroom soup
- 250 ml water
- 250 ml cream
- 5 ml salt
- finely chopped chives
- 5 ml black pepper

Wash and drain meat well. Combine all spices and add to meat; leave for 30 minutes to absorb flavour.

Melt butter in a pan and cook meat for 20 minutes, adding extra water, a little at a time, till soft and cooked.

Cook pasta till *al dente* in rapidly boiling water, adding salt and oil.

Drain; then toss with oil and keep aside.

In a large pan, melt butter. Add onion and sauté until golden and soft, about 10 minutes. Add water if necessary. Add mushrooms and stir–fry.

Mix together soup, water and cream. Add soup mix to the pan; simmer gently into a thick sauce. Season with salt and pepper according to taste.

Add cooked meat and sauce to pasta and toss well. Garnish with chives and black pepper. Serve immediately.

Serves 6–8

Cubed steak with creamy mushroom and penne

MINCE LASAGNE TOPPED WITH CHEESE
Melting, creamy and simply delicious

- 150 g green lasagna sheets
- 1 medium onion, chopped
- 15 ml crushed garlic
- 30 ml olive or cooking oil
- 750 g beef mince
- 1 can tomato and onion mix
- 30 ml tomato paste
- 5 ml salt
- 5 ml black pepper
- 15 ml barbeque spice
- 15 ml paprika
- 5 ml peri–peri powder

White sauce
- 50 g butter
- 50 g cake flour
- 500 ml milk
- 5 ml salt
- 3 ml white pepper

Topping
- 250 ml grated cheese
- finely chopped parsley

Lasagne sheets
Steep 3 sheets into boiling water one by one (otherwise the sheets will stick to one another) and boil for 10 minutes until tender. Drain well and spread onto oiled greaseproof paper. Repeat until all sheets are cooked.

Meat sauce
Heat oil; braise onion and garlic in a large saucepan.

Add mince, tomato and onion mix, tomato paste, spices and season well. Cover with lid and cook gently.

White sauce
Melt the butter in a saucepan over low heat. Stir in flour, salt and pepper. Gradually add milk and bring to the boil, stirring until sauce is smooth.

Assembly
Grease an oven–proof dish well. Place layer of lasagna sheets on the base of dish. Spread meat sauce over sheets. Then spread some white sauce over meat followed by another layer of lasagna sheets.

Continue layering in this manner, ending with a layer of white sauce.

Sprinkle with cheese and parsley and bake for 30–40 minutes at 180 °C until cheese is golden and the dish is heated through.

Leave to settle and then cut into portions.

Serves 6–8

Mince lasagne topped with cheese

HERBED CHICKEN WITH BOWTIE PASTA

Sweet and tantalising with a fresh herby taste

- 300 g bowtie pasta
- 60 ml cooking oil
- 1 onion, finely chopped
- 500 g chicken fillets, thinly sliced
- 10 ml dried tarragon
- 45 ml crushed garlic
- 45 ml chicken spice
- 10 ml coarse black pepper
- 200 g sundried tomatoes, cut in half
- salt to taste
- 250 g baby tomatoes, left whole
- 15 black olives
- 30 ml honey
- 5 ml cayenne pepper
- fresh herbs of choice for garnish

Boil pasta until *al dente* in salted boiling water. Drain and keep aside.

In a large pot, heat oil with onion; braise well till golden. Add chicken and all spices. Toss well and stir-fry for 7 minutes.

Add sundried tomatoes and season with salt. In a large bowl, combine pasta and chicken mixture; toss well.

Add baby tomatoes, olives, honey and seasoning. Place in an oven-proof dish and bake in a preheated oven at 180 °C for about 15 minutes.

Garnish with herbs and serve hot with crusty bread.

Serves 6–8

PASTA WITH CHILLI, ORANGE AND CRUNCHY GREEN VEG

Spicy and sweet with a crunchy fresh texture

- 250 g spiral pasta
- 45 ml oil
- 30 ml crushed garlic
- 15 ml whole cumin seeds
- 5 ml crushed whole coriander seeds
- 1 large green pepper, chopped
- 5 celery sticks, chopped
- 2 green chillies, chopped
- 10 ml Cajun spice
- 5 ml salt
- 3 ml white pepper
- 10 ml orange rind
- 60 ml fresh orange juice
- 60 ml chopped green dhania
- 100 ml salad dressing of choice

Cook pasta in boiling water until *al dente*. Toss in cooking oil and keep warm. Cover with a lid.

Heat oil in a large pot. Add garlic and seeds and braise till aroma escapes.

Add rest of ingredients, except salad dressing, and stir-fry for 2 minutes (do not over-cook; veggies must still be crisp-crunchy). Adjust seasoning, if necessary.

Toss vegetable mix together with pasta; add salad dressing and combine well. Heat through briefly.

Serve with asparagus and fresh orange segments on the side.

Serves 6–8

SPAGHETTI MINCE PIE
A mince pie on a spaghetti base topped with cheese

Base
- 100 ml butter or margarine, softened
- 200 g spaghetti
- 100 ml grated cheese
- 3 eggs, beaten
- seasoning as desired

Filling
- 40 ml butter or margarine
- 2 medium onions, chopped
- 1 green pepper, chopped
- 10 ml crushed garlic
- 750 g minced beef
- 3 tomatoes, grated
- 10 ml barbeque spice
- 5 ml paprika
- 5 ml salt
- 5 ml pepper
- 20 ml tomato purée
- 200 g grated cheese, for topping

Boil spaghetti as per instructions on the pack and keep aside. Coat a flan dish with non-stick cooking spray.

Combine butter or margarine with spaghetti, cheese and egg. Spread mixture over base and sides of flan dishes to form a crust. Season base as desired.

Preheat oven to 180 °C.

Heat butter or margarine in a saucepan. Add onions, green pepper and garlic. Sauté until onion is transparent and very soft and golden. Add mince, tomatoes and spices. Add purée and cook, stirring constantly, adding a little water if necessary.

Cool mixture for 5–10 minutes and spoon into shell. Bake for 20–25 minutes. Sprinkle pie with cheese and continue to bake until cheese is melted and golden.

Remove from oven and allow to rest for 10 minutes before cutting into wedges.

Serve with green salad and crusty bread.

Serves 6–8

MUSHROOM LEMON RICE
Tangy and spicy

- 500 ml long–grain white rice
- 1 litre water
- 5 ml salt
- 30 ml sunflower oil
- 1 small onion, finely chopped
- 30 ml crushed garlic
- 200 g mushrooms, finely sliced
- 5 ml paprika
- 5 ml white pepper
- 5 ml rice spice
- 10 ml lemon rind
- salt to taste
- chopped dhania for garnish

Boil rice in salted boiling water until tender, but not soft. Rinse under cold running water and allow to drain.

Meanwhile, add oil to a non–stick pot. Add onion and garlic; sauté for a few seconds to release the aroma of the garlic. Add the mushrooms and stir–fry for 5 minutes.

Add rice, spices and lemon rind. Stir through and allow to steam over gentle heat until rice is heated through.

Garnish with sliced mushrooms and finely chopped dhania.

Serves 6–8

SWEET SAFFRON RICE
A delicately flavoured rice

- 500 ml basmati rice
- 1.5 litre water
- salt to taste
- 2 cinnamon sticks
- 4 cardamom pods
- 5 saffron strands
- 65 ml sugar
- 100 g butter or margarine

Soak the basmati rice in cold water for 30 minutes, then rinse.

Bring the water, salt, cinnamon and cardamom pods to the boil. Add the rice and bring to the boil.

Turn down the heat and simmer for 10–12 minutes, or until the rice is still firm in the middle of the grain. Remove from the pan and rinse well under cold water. Drain.

Return to the saucepan and add the saffron, sugar and butter or margarine. Stir together gently.

Cover with a tightly fitting lid and steam gently for 15–20 minutes.

Serves 6–8

Mushroom lemon rice

TUNA TAGLIATELLE WITH SAFFRON SAUCE
Pasta in a creamy saffron sauce

- 250 g tagliatelle
- 1 medium onion, finely chopped
- 45 ml oil
- 25 ml crushed garlic
- 2 chillies, chopped
- 1 large tomato, finely grated
- 45 ml tomato paste
- 2 tins tuna, drained and flaked
- 15 ml barbecue spice
- 10 ml sugar (optional)
- few strands of saffron
- 250 ml fresh cream
- 10 ml paprika
- salt to taste
- pepper to taste
- parsley for garnish

Cook pasta according to instructions on pack until *al dente*.

In a frying pan, heat oil; add onion and sauté until soft.

Stir in garlic, chillies, tomato and tomato paste. Simmer for 20–30 minutes.

Stir in tuna, add barbeque spice and season to taste with salt. Add sugar if necessary.

Dry-roast saffron strands in a pan and keep aside.

Heat pasta with cream and saffron in a separate pot. Season with paprika, salt and pepper.

Toss tuna mixture into pasta sauce and garnish with parsley sprigs.

Serve with salad and crusty bread.

Serves 6–8

PASTA ALFREDO
Penne pasta with a fresh mushroom cream sauce

- 300 g penne pasta
- 50 g butter
- 1 medium onion, chopped
- 200 g mushrooms, sliced
- 5 ml black pepper
- 30 ml barbecue spice
- 30 ml garlic paste
- 10 ml salt
- 500 ml fresh cream
- finely chopped parsley and fresh green chilli for garnish

Cook pasta as per instructions on pack, until *al dente*. Drain, toss with a little oil and keep aside.

Melt butter in saucepan. Add onion and cook for 10 minutes, or until soft and golden.

Add mushrooms. Sauté for 5 minutes. Add spices and garlic, sauté for 2 minutes. Season to taste.

Add cream and heat to boiling point, stirring until thick and creamy.

Add sauce to pasta and serve garnished with chopped parsley, fresh chilli and ground black pepper.

Serves 4–6

Hint: Add fresh milk to sauce if necessary to thin sauce down.

Pasta Alfredo

YELLOW SWEET RICE
Delightfully sweet and fruity

- 1.5 litre water
- 500 ml long–grain white rice
- 5 ml salt

Syrup
- 50 ml butter
- 2 cinnamon sticks
- 4 cardamom pods
- 100 ml sultanas
- 200 ml water
- 50 ml sugar
- 5 ml salt
- 2 ml yellow food colouring

In a large pot, bring water to the boil. Rinse rice and add to boiling water. Add salt and cook, uncovered, until tender. Rinse under cold running water and allow to drain in colander.

In a pot, melt butter with cinnamon and cardamom till bubbly. Add sultanas and braise for 2 minutes. Add water and bring to the boil. Add sugar, salt and food colouring. Allow to simmer for 10–15 minutes.

Mix in rice and steam over low heat for 10 minutes, tossing lightly with a fork every now and then.

Serve with roasts.

Serves 6–8

SAVOURY RICE
A good old family favourite

- 500 ml long–grain white rice
- about 1 litre water
- 5 ml salt
- 30 ml sunflower oil
- 1 small onion, finely chopped
- 30 ml crushed garlic
- 250 g frozen mixed vegetables
- 5 ml paprika
- 5 ml peri–peri powder
- 10 ml rice spice
- salt to taste
- baby corn and chopped dhania for garnish

Boil rice in salted boiling water until tender, but not soft. Place under cold running water and allow to drain.

Meanwhile, add oil to a non–stick pot. Add onion and garlic and sauté for a few seconds to release the aroma of the garlic.

Add frozen vegetables and stir–fry for 3–5 minutes. Add rice and spices. Stir through and allow to steam over gentle heat until rice is heated through. Season with extra salt if necessary.

Garnish with baby corn and green dhania.

Serves 6–8

ROASTED SAFFRON AND COCONUT RICE RING
A feast for the eye

- 300 g Tastic rice
- 5 ml turmeric
- salt to taste
- 60 ml butter
- 1 medium onion, finely chopped
- 100 ml coconut milk
- 1 red pepper, chopped
- 2 green chillies
- 30 ml garlic paste
- 30 ml rice spice
- 10 ml paprika
- 100 ml roasted coconut
- ½ bunch fresh dhania, chopped
- 2 ml saffron, roasted (keep aside)

Spray a glass pyrex ring mould with non–stick cooking spray.

Boil rice as per instructions on pack; add turmeric and salt. Drain and keep aside.

In a separate pot, melt butter and add onion; braise till transparent but not brown.

Add coconut milk and heat for 2 minutes. Add all ingredients and stir–fry for 3–5 minutes. Stir in cooked rice and heat through well.

Heat saffron in a small pan till fragrant. Crush saffron with fingers and sprinkle into ring mould. Place rice mixture into mould and press down firmly. Take care that rice is pressed down really well and do not use a ring that is too big for the rice mixture. Leave to set for a few minutes.

Turn out into a large serving platter, shaking dish slightly to release rice and garnish with a sprig of fresh dhania. Serve this attractive centrepiece with roast chicken and salad.

Serves 6–8

COCONUT AND ALMOND RICE
A deliciously nutty fried rice

- 750 ml white fragrant rice, uncooked
- 250 ml coconut milk
- boiling water
- salt to taste
- 45 ml butter or margarine

For frying rice
- 60 ml butter
- 60 ml coconut milk
- 60 ml coarse coconut
- 100 ml ground almonds

This recipe uses the absorption method to cook the rice.

Boil all ingredients for rice together till water and coconut milk is absorbed. Do not drain off any water; use only as required.

Steam till done, fluffing rice from time to time.

To fry rice
Coat a wok with non–stick cooking spray. Heat butter in wok; melt and add coconut milk, coconut and almonds. Braise for 1–2 minutes. Toss rice in and very lightly fry over high heat till well–coated and fragrant. Take care that rice does not stick to wok.

Serves 6–8

SWEET AND SOUR CHICKEN
Simply mouth-watering

- 30 ml oil
- 4 chicken breasts
- 1 white onion, sliced
- 1 red onion, sliced
- 2 red peppers, cubed
- 2 green peppers, cubed
- 1 pineapple, cubed
- 2 spring onions, julienned
- 1 green chilli, finely chopped
- 30 ml garlic paste
- 5 ml salt
- 5 ml pepper
- 30 ml Cajun spice
- 100 ml sweet chilli sauce
- 30 ml lemon juice
- 300 g cooked spaghetti
- spring onion for garnishing

Heat oil in a wok. Add chicken and cook for 5–7 minutes.

Add sliced onions, peppers, pineapple, spring onions, chilli and garlic and stir–fry for 5 minutes.

Add salt, pepper, Cajun spice, sweet chilli sauce and lemon juice; cook for 3–5 minutes.

Place on cooked spaghetti, garnish with spring onion and serve hot.

Serves 6–8

BOWTIES WITH SALMON SAUCE
Pasta in a light creamy sauce

- 250 g bowtie pasta
- 1 medium onion, chopped
- 500 ml parsley, firmly packed
- 20 ml crushed garlic
- 250 ml grated cheese (optional)
- 250 ml creamy salad dressing of your choice
- 2 cans salmon, flaked
- 15 ml lemon juice
- 15 ml cayenne pepper
- 45 ml fish spice
- salt and pepper to taste
- cheese for sprinkling (optional)

Cook pasta according to the instructions on the pack till *al dente*.

In a food processor, combine onion, parsley, garlic and cheese (if using).

In a steady stream, add salad dressing to food processor, blending until mixture thickens. Transfer mixture to a large saucepan.

Add fish, spices and lemon juice.

Heat mixture over low heat for 4–5 minutes for flavours to blend.

Add pasta and toss to coat. Season according to personal preference.

Pile into a warmed dish and serve while still warm.

Serves 6–8

Sweet and sour chicken

CHICKEN AND SPINACH LASAGNE
A creamy, delectable dish

- 1 packet egg lasagna sheets
- 60 ml cooking or olive oil
- 2 medium onions, finely chopped
- 60 ml crushed garlic
- 2 green chillies, chopped
- 1 green pepper, chopped
- 1 kg coarse chicken mince
- 30 ml chicken spice
- 15 ml paprika
- 15 ml coarse lemon pepper
- 30 ml Portuguese spice
- 1 punnet mushrooms, sliced
- 1 bunch spinach, shredded

Sauce
- 100 g butter or margarine
- 30 ml garlic paste
- 100 g cake flour
- 750 ml milk
- 5 ml white pepper
- salt to taste
- 250 ml water

Topping
- 250 ml grated cheese
- fresh parsley, finely chopped

Lasagne sheets
Steep sheets in boiling water one by one and cook for 10 minutes until *al dente*. Drain well and spread onto oiled greaseproof paper. Lasagne sheets must be cooked 3 at a time otherwise the sheets will stick to one another.

In a separate pot, add oil and braise onions, garlic and chillies till soft. Add green pepper, chicken mince and all spices. Stir–fry for 5–7 minutes, adding 50 ml water if necessary. Add mushrooms and spinach and cook for a further 3 minutes. Remove and keep aside.

Sauce
Melt butter or margarine in a medium–sized pot, stir in garlic and sift in flour. Cook for 1 minute. Remove from heat and stir in milk. Season with salt and pepper. Place on stove and continue to stir (do not let any lumps form; if it's not a smooth sauce, use an egg beater at this stage). Bring to the boil till mixture thickens. Add some water if too thick.

Assembly
Use a large oven–proof dish and layer some lasagne sheets at the base of dish. Top with chicken filling, then a layer of sauce. Repeat layering, ending off with white sauce. Sprinkle with cheese and parsley.

Bake, uncovered at 180 °C for about 45 minutes, or until top is golden.

Serve with a salad of choice.

Serves 8–10

NOODLE AND VIENNA CHEESE BAKE
An easy but very tasty, economical dish

- 300 g screw noodles
- 10 ml oil
- 1 medium onion, finely chopped
- 1 green chilli, finely chopped
- 10 ml garlic paste
- 3 tomatoes, skinned and finely chopped
- 30 ml tomato purée
- 5 ml sugar
- 5 ml pepper
- 15 ml Portuguese spice
- 10 ml barbecue spice
- 10 Vienna sausages, cut into pieces
- 250 ml grated cheese
- salt to taste

Preheat oven to 180°C. Prepare an oven–proof dish by coating with non–stick cooking spray.

Bring 4 litres of water to the boil. Add noodles with 15 ml salt and cook till *al dente*. Drain. Drizzle with oil, mix through and keep aside.

Meanwhile, sauté onion in oil until golden, adding water if necessary.

Add chilli and garlic; sauté for 1 minute. Add chopped tomatoes, tomato purée, sugar and seasonings. Simmer for 8–10 minutes.

Add Viennas and cook for 2 minutes extra. Toss in pasta. Place noodle mixture into the dish and sprinkle with grated cheese.

Bake in the oven for about 10 minutes, or until heated through and cheese is golden brown.

Serves 6–8

PASTA WITH CHICKEN, MUSHROOM, CHILLI AND CHUTNEY
Tangy, spicy and flavoursome

- 250 g macaroni pasta
- 15 ml butter
- 1 medium onion, finely chopped
- 60 ml crushed garlic
- 1 medium green pepper, diced
- 100 g mushrooms, sliced
- 500 g chicken breasts, cubed
- 1 can tomato and onion mix
- 30 ml tomato purée
- 60 ml chilli sauce
- 60 ml chutney
- 30 ml chicken spice
- 30 ml tandoori spice
- 5 ml white pepper
- 10 ml sugar
- salt to taste
- 250 ml grated cheese

Cook pasta according to instructions on pack until *al dente*.

Meanwhile, heat butter and fry onion until lightly golden. Add garlic, green pepper and mushrooms; fry for 3 minutes.

Add chicken and fry until cooked through. Add tomato and onion mix, sauces, spices, sugar and salt. Simmer for 5–7 minutes, until sauce thickens.

Mix drained pasta with sauce. Combine well and spoon into oven–proof dish.

Sprinkle with grated cheese and bake at 180 °C until cheese has melted and is golden.

Serve with crusty bread and a green salad.

Serves 6–8

Pasta with chicken, mushroom, chilli and chutney

CHAPTER FIVE

Fish — Bounty of the Sea

Fish is the bounty of the Cape's
oceans, a valuable source of
protein and vitamins.
The versatility of seafood lends itself
to a boundless array of flavours
and aromas.

CREAMY COCONUT FISH CURRY
Smooth, tangy and creamy

- 1 kg cob, yellowtail or snoek
- 3 large tomatoes, chopped
- 30 ml crushed garlic
- 20 ml cayenne pepper
- 5 ml turmeric
- 30 ml fish masala
- 15 ml salt, or to taste
- 60 ml water
- 200 ml coconut milk
- 45 ml oil
- 5 curry leaves
- 3 whole green chillies
- 45 ml finely chopped dhania for garnishing

Wash and drain fish.

Liquidise tomatoes, garlic, spices, salt, water and coconut milk.

Add oil to a pot with a wide enough bottom to allow fish to lie in a single layer.

Add curry leaves and chillies, and fry over medium heat until slightly brown and aromatic.

Pour liquidised tomato into pot and allow to simmer for 5 minutes until sauce has thickened and reduced.

Place fish in pot and simmer till cooked, for about 10 minutes.

Remove from heat, garnish with dhania and serve with white rice, poppadums and onion salad.

Variations:
- Add mustard seeds to oil with curry leaves and allow to splatter to release the flavour of the seeds.
- When quince is in season, peel and slice. Boil in lightly salted water until soft. Drain and add to fish.
- Slice and rinse brinjal with salted water. Bring to the boil in lightly salted water and cook until soft. Drain. Add to fish.
- Add green mango to curry before fish and let it cook as usual.

Serves 4–6

SPICY SWEET AND SOUR FISH BAKE
A tasty blend of tamarind and spices

- 1 kg fish cutlets of choice
- 45 ml cooking oil
- 30 ml butter
- 10 curry leaves
- 100 g tamarind
- 125 ml warm water
- 5 ml turmeric
- 45 ml tandoori masala
- 10 ml paprika powder
- 30 ml garlic paste
- 10 ml salt
- 60 ml tomato purée
- 60 ml brown sugar
- chopped dhania and tomato for garnishing

Preheat oven to 180°C. In a large oven-proof dish, place oil and butter. Heat and add curry leaves.

In a small bowl, steep tamarind in warm water. Squeeze out the pulp and discard the pips. In a bowl, place tamarind and add all the remaining ingredients.

Mix into a paste. Rub spice over the fish and place in the hot butter mixture.

Bake for 10–12 minutes and turn oven temperature up to grill, leaving fish to grill for 8–10 minutes.

Garnish with fresh dhania and tomato. Serve with masala potatoes and crusty bread.

Serves 4–6

Creamy coconut fish curry

TUNA BREYANI
A tasty, versatile dish

- 100 ml oil, for frying of potatoes
- 4 large potatoes, sliced
- 2 large onions, thinly sliced
- 30 ml butter, for braising vegetables
- 15 ml garlic paste
- 5 ml cayenne pepper
- 30 ml fish spice
- 15 ml jeera powder
- 10 ml koljana powder
- 15 ml garlic paste
- 300 g frozen mixed vegetables
- 3 cans tuna, drained and flaked, or 2 cans salmon
- 750 ml cooked long–grain rice
- 50 ml butter, to dab on top of onion layer
- 60 ml hot water, coloured with 2 ml yellow food colouring
- 4 hard–boiled eggs, halved
- fresh chopped dhania for garnishing

Heat oil in large frying pad and fry potato slices on each side until golden brown. Drain and set aside.

In same oil, fry onions until golden. Drain and keep aside.

In a clean pan, melt 30 ml butter with garlic over medium heat.

Add spices and vegetables; cook for 5 minutes and remove from heat. Gently mix in tuna with fork.

In a large glass casserole dish, using half the potatoes and rice, place a layer of potatoes and then a layer of rice. Top with tuna mixture.

Layer with rest of potatoes and rice, ending with rice.

Sprinkle with fried onions and dot with butter. Sprinkle with coloured water and place in oven at 180 °C to heat through.

Garnish with boiled eggs and dhania.

Serves 6–8

Note: Do not pour left–over oil over rice.

Tuna breyani

GRILLED TANDOORI PRAWNS
Simply tantalising

- 1 kg tiger prawns
- 45 ml garlic paste
- 60 ml tandoori spice
- 10 ml cracked whole coriander seeds
- 60 ml lemon juice
- 60 ml finely chopped fresh dhania
- 60 ml cooking oil
- 100 ml butter
- 10 curry leaves

Place prawns in a bowl. In a separate small bowl, combine the garlic and all the spices, and mix with lemon juice, dhania and cooking oil.

Add the marinade to the prawns and toss. Leave for about 1 hour.

In a large oven–proof dish, place the butter and curry leaves. Heat well, melting the butter completely.

Place prawns in the dish in neat rows and grill for 8–10 minutes. Turn prawns over with a fork and grill for a further 5 minutes, basting with the butter if necessary.

Serve on a roti with spicy vegetables and pickle.

Serves 4–6

PICKLED FISH
A traditional pickled fish dish

- 1 kg kabeljou, cut into portions
- 30 ml fish spice
- 5 ml salt
- 10 ml white pepper
- oil for frying

Curry sauce
- 6 large onions, sliced
- 15 ml oil
- 4 cloves garlic, crushed
- 400 ml brown vinegar
- 60 ml sugar (more if desired)
- 30 ml turmeric
- 60 ml curry powder
- 30 ml cayenne pepper
- 20 ml fish spice
- 5 bay leaves
- 6 whole allspice
- 4 dried red chillies (optional)
- salt to taste

Season fish with spice, salt and pepper.

Fry fish in hot oil for 5 minutes on each side or until medium brown and cooked through. Remove from oil and drain on absorbent paper.

To make the curry sauce, cook onions, oil, vinegar and all the spices in a saucepan until well blended; 15–20 minutes. Add salt to taste.

Place fish slices in a deep dish and cover with the sauce. Store, covered, in refrigerator for 24 hours before serving, to allow the flavours to develop.

Serves 8–10

Grilled tandoori prawns

CRAYFISH CURRY
Spicy, tangy, simply delicious

- 8 cleaned and deveined crayfish tails
- 3 tomatoes, chopped
- 20 ml crushed garlic
- 20 ml cayenne pepper
- 20 ml seafood masala
- 5 ml jeera powder
- 15 ml turmeric
- 5 ml salt, or to taste
- 100 ml water
- 45 ml oil
- 5 curry leaves
- 5 whole cloves
- 5 ml black mustard seeds (optional)
- 200 ml coconut milk
- 45 ml finely chopped dhania
- 2 green chillies

Wash and drain the crayfish tails.

Liquidise tomatoes, garlic, spices, salt and water.

Over medium heat, add oil to a pot. The pot should ideally have a wide bottom to allow crayfish to lie in a single layer.

Add curry leaves, whole cloves and mustard seeds; fry until slightly brown and aromatic.

Pour liquidised tomato into pot and allow to simmer for 15 minutes until sauce is thickened and reduced.

Place crayfish in pot and simmer till cooked and shell is red in colour; about 10 minutes.

Add coconut milk and stir well. Heat through; remove from heat and garnish with dhania and chopped green chillies.

Serve with white basmati rice, poppadums and onion salad.

Serves 4–6

PRAWN CHAAT
A sheer indulgence

- 1 kg tiger prawns, deveined, shell intact
- 15 ml garlic paste
- 10 ml seafood masala
- 5 ml salt
- 10 ml lemon juice
- 60 ml cooking oil
- 30 ml butter

Sauce
- 100 ml water
- 30 ml seafood masala
- 30 ml jeera powder
- 10 ml crushed chillies
- 2 ml red powder food colouring
- 2 ml yellow food colouring
- 5 ml salt
- 250 ml plain yoghurt
- 15 ml butter
- 6 curry leaves
- 250 ml fresh cream
- chopped dhania for garnishing

Combine garlic paste, masala, salt and lemon juice in a large bowl. Marinate prawns for 15 minutes.

Heat oil and butter in a large pan. Fry prawns a few at a time till pink in colour. Set aside when all prawns are cooked.

Make sauce by blending together 100 ml water, seafood masala, jeera powder, crushed chillies, food colouring, salt and yoghurt.

In a large flat pot, melt butter and add curry leaves; sauté lightly till aroma escapes. Add yoghurt mixture and keep on stirring till mixture boils. The sauce should be creamy and slightly pink. Remove from heat; add cream and stir well. Add prawns to sauce and simmer over low heat for 3–5 minutes.

Garnish with fresh dhania. Serve with naan bread, poppadums and an onion and tomato salad.

Serves 6–8

Crayfish curry

Fish

GRILLED KINGKLIP STUFFED WITH SPINACH AND FETA
A creamy lemony-flavoured fish with an amazing filling

- 2 lemons (grate rind and squeeze out juice)
- 30 ml fish spice
- 15 ml crushed garlic
- 15 ml paprika
- coarsely milled black pepper
- 15 ml Worcestershire sauce or soy sauce
- 1 kg thick kingklip, filleted cutlets
- 60 ml butter
- 30 ml oil

Stuffing
- ½ bunch spinach, chopped coarsely
- 3 rounds feta cheese, crumbled
- 5 ml fish spice

Topping (optional)
- 50 ml cake flour
- 50 g butter
- 5 ml salt
- 5 ml pepper
- 500 ml milk

Mix the lemon juice, fish spice, garlic, paprika, black pepper and Worcestershire or soy sauce into a marinade. Smear marinade over fish and set aside, preferably overnight for a better flavour.

Steam spinach and squeeze to remove excess water. Mix together spinach, feta and fish spice; keep aside.

If topping is desired, place the ingredients into a pot and whisk together thoroughly over medium heat. Continue whisking until mixture thickens. Once thickened, allow to boil for 1 minute. If topping is too thick, thin it down with a little milk. Set aside until needed.

Heat oven to grill and place shelf in centre of oven. Coat an oblong glass dish with non-stick cooking spray. Place butter and oil in dish and keep aside.

Remove fish from marinade and place on a sheet of greaseproof paper. Slice each cutlet through by filleting open three-quarters of the way. Stuff each filleted piece with spinach and feta mixture. Close fish slice and press neatly together. Complete all the slices.

Place dish in the oven till butter is hot and sizzling. Remove from oven and neatly pack fish in dish, scooping a little melted butter over the cutlets.

Place dish back in the oven and grill for 10–15 minutes till fish is white and flaky.

Remove from oven and pour topping sauce over the fish. Sprinkle with lemon rind and return to oven. Lower heat to 180 °C and bake for 5 minutes till white sauce is heated through.

Serve with rice and roasted veggies.

Serves 4–6

Note: Use topping if a creamy dish is desired.

88

Grilled kingklip stuffed with spinach and feta

ALMOND FISH BAKE
An unusual baked fish with a delicious crusty topping

- 5 ml turmeric
- 5 ml cayenne pepper
- 2 chillies, finely chopped
- 30 ml koljana powder
- 15 ml jeera powder
- 40 ml crushed garlic
- 5 ml salt
- 15 ml lemon juice
- 1 small onion, grated
- 1 kg white fish of choice
- 125 ml oil
- 1 large onion, sliced
- 3 tomatoes, grated
- 100 ml coconut milk
- 125 ml slivered almonds
- finely chopped dhania for garnishing

Preheat oven to 180 °C.

Mix spices, garlic, salt, lemon juice and grated onion with a teaspoon of oil. Keep aside a quarter of the spice mix and smear rest of mixture well over the fish.

Add half the oil to a heatproof dish. Place fish in dish and bake for 20–30 minutes, or until almost done.

Meanwhile, fry sliced onion in remaining oil. When onion begins to change colour, add the grated tomatoes, coconut milk and remaining spice mix.

Lower the heat and allow to simmer for a few minutes till curry is nicely blended.

Pour the curry mixture over the fish. Garnish with slivered almonds and bake till fish is done.

Garnish with finely chopped dhania. Serve with braised onion rice or rotis.

Serves 4–6

HADDOCK KEDGEREE
A stunning combination of yellow, green and white

- 1 kg smoked haddock
- 2 medium onions, finely chopped
- 60 ml butter
- 30 ml cooking oil
- 30 ml crushed garlic
- 30 ml paprika
- 30 ml fish spice
- 5 ml peri–peri powder
- 7 ml salt
- 5 ml pepper
- 500 ml steamed rice
- 250 ml frozen peas, steamed
- 6 hard–boiled eggs, sliced
- 30 ml chopped fresh dhania
- 2 ml yellow food colouring, mixed with 125 ml water
- 15 ml butter, to dab after assembling dish

Cut haddock into large chunks. Arrange haddock on a prepared warm oven tray and place in oven at 180 °C for 10–15 minutes or until cooked through.

Remove from oven and keep aside. Braise onions in a pot with butter and oil until golden; add garlic and all spices, cook for a minute or two to release aroma. Remove from heat and leave aside.

Place cooked rice at the bottom of a flat oven–proof dish. Sprinkle with a layer of peas. Place hard–boiled eggs on top of the peas. Then layer with the haddock. Place braised spiced onion over haddock. Sprinkle with dhania.

Cut the butter into small cubes and place on the haddock mixture.

Sprinkle with yellow water and place in the oven for 15–20 minutes or until heated through.

Serve with roast potatoes or a green salad.

Serves 6–8

Haddock kedgeree

CHAPTER SIX

Sumptuous Chicken

A clever combination of
ingredients, creative seasonings
and interesting cooking methods
make chicken one of the most
versatile highlights of a main meal.
Intense pleasure and nostalgia are
created by visualising pot–roast
chicken with potatoes, smothered in
finger–licking sauces.

CHICKEN IN COCONUT CURRY WITH CHUNKY VEGETABLES

A rich curry served with chunky vegetables in an array of colours

- 1 whole chicken, cut into pieces
- 10 ml turmeric
- 5 ml jeera powder
- 10 ml koljana powder
- 15 ml garlic and ginger paste
- 10 ml barbeque spice
- 10 ml salt
- 60 ml butter or margarine
- 15 ml cooking oil
- 250 ml water
- 410 g can coconut milk mixed with 1 cup water
- ½ bunch green dhania leaves, chopped
- 100 ml water (optional)

Vegetables

- 30 ml extra butter or margarine
- 8 baby marrows, halved
- 200 g mushrooms, halved
- 2 punnets baby corn
- 12 baby carrots, left whole
- 12 green beans, topped and tailed, cut in half
- 1 green pepper, quartered
- 1 red pepper, quartered

Wash and drain chicken well. Mix all spices and seasoning together with a little water. Smear spices over chicken and marinate for a few hours or overnight.

In a large flat pot, melt butter or margarine and oil over medium heat. Add chicken and brown on both sides for a few minutes.

Add 250 ml water and continue to cook, taking care not to stir chicken too much. Rather shake the pot. This is to prevent the chicken from breaking. Remove chicken and keep aside.

In same pot, add the extra butter and start stir-frying vegetables in batches. Stir-fry for 3–4 minutes until all vegetables are done. Remove from pot.

Add coconut milk and water. Bring to the boil and add chicken to create a layer on the base of the pot. Add vegetables and heat through. If a thicker consistency is required, mix together 15 ml cornflour and 30 ml water and add to the chicken.

Serve with fragrant white rice.

Serves 6–8

Note: Any vegetables of your choice may be used. But, remember to cut them into large chunks and have different colours and textures.

Chicken in coconut curry with chunky vegetables

SOUTH INDIAN BUTTER CHICKEN
The traditional butter chicken

- 60 g butter
- 15 ml oil
- 1 kg chicken fillets, cut into cubes
- 2 medium onions, finely chopped
- 20 ml garam masala
- 20 ml koljana powder
- 20 ml garlic and ginger paste
- 10 ml jeera powder
- 20 ml cayenne pepper
- 5 ml salt
- 3 cardamom pods
- 5 black peppercorns
- 150 ml natural yoghurt
- 60 ml tomato purée
- 150 ml milk or water
- 3 curry leaves
- 15 ml cornflour
- 200 ml cream
- fresh coriander
- green onions

Heat butter and oil in a pot. Sear the chicken pieces until they are brown. Remove from pot.

In same pot, fry onions until they are golden and soft, adding a little water to cook onions till soft.

In a separate bowl, blend together all the spices, yoghurt, tomato purée and chicken pieces. Add this to the onions.

Add the milk and curry leaves and simmer for 15 minutes, stirring occasionally. Mix the cornflour with the cream and add to the chicken.

Cook for a further 10–15 minutes. Garnish with fresh coriander and chopped green onions.

Serve with naan bread.

Serves 6–8

South Indian butter chicken

WHOLE ROASTED ORANGE AND APRICOT-GLAZED CHICKEN
A tangy taste that lingers on

- 1 whole chicken, cleaned and dried
- 30 ml chicken spice
- 1 orange, peeled and cut into segments
- 200 ml apricot jam
- 1 lemon, juiced
- 30 ml garlic and ginger paste
- 15 ml peri–peri powder
- 15 ml chicken spice
- 15 ml paprika
- 5 ml salt
- 5 ml pepper

Preheat oven to 200 °C. Rub the 30 ml chicken spice over and inside the cavity of chicken.

Place orange segments into chicken cavity. Mix remaining ingredients to make a basting sauce.

Place chicken in a roasting pan and liberally brush with basting sauce.

Cover chicken with foil, shiny side in, and bake for 30 minutes.

Reduce oven temperature to 180 °C and roast, covered, for a further 30 minutes. Remove foil and roast until golden, basting every now and again.

Garnish with orange wedges and serve with rice, and baked or steamed veggies.

Serves 6–8

GRILLED CHICKEN TIKKA PIECES
A spicy dish flavoured with lemon and yoghurt

- 1 whole chicken, cut into pieces

Marinade
- 30 ml oil
- 200 ml low fat plain yoghurt
- 30 ml garlic and ginger paste
- 30 ml lemon juice
- 60 ml tandoori spice
- 10 ml garam masala
- 30 ml cayenne pepper
- 20 ml cornflour
- salt to taste

Baste
- 30 ml butter or margarine, melted
- 20 ml garlic

Mix together all marinade ingredients in a bowl. Add chicken and stir through thoroughly, coating all the chicken pieces.

Cover and allow to marinate for 5–6 hours or overnight in refrigerator.

Braai or grill, turning and basting every few minutes until cooked but still juicy; about 20–30 minutes.

Serve as a main course with salads or chutneys, rice and vegetables of choice.

Serves 6–8

CHICKEN KEBABS
Tangy chicken on a skewer

- 1 kg chicken breast fillets
- 5 ml salt
- 5 ml cayenne pepper
- 2.5 ml jeera powder
- 5 ml pepper
- 20 ml lemon juice
- 1 green pepper, cut into big cubes
- 1 punnet button mushrooms, halved
- 100 g pickling onions, peeled and halved
- 30 ml cooking oil
- 30 ml butter, melted
- skewers for threading kebabs

Set oven to grill. Cube chicken fillets. Wash and drain well. Combine chicken with salt, spices and lemon juice in a large bowl. Mix well.

Cover and allow to marinate. Thread chicken onto skewers which have been pre–soaked in water, alternating with green pepper, mushroom and onion.

Place on an oven tray covered with foil. Grill kebabs, basting with mixture of oil and butter repeatedly, and turn kebabs until chicken is cooked through.

Serve on a bed of fresh salad.

Serves 6–8

Note: As a variation, use dried fruit or any other vegetable of choice.

GRILLED WHOLE TANDOORI CHICKEN
The 'secret' is in the spice

- 1 whole chicken, cleaned and washed
- 30 ml paprika
- 10 ml cayenne pepper
- 30 ml coriander seeds, finely crushed
- 20 ml crushed chillies
- 45 ml freshly chopped garlic
- 10 ml salt
- 60 ml lemon juice
- 40 ml butter or margarine, melted
- tomatoes, cut into wedges

Preheat oven to 180 °C. Clean chicken and pat dry. Cut chicken spatchcock style (halve from breast side).

Make a marinade with all the spices, garlic, salt and lemon juice. Smear over chicken and marinade for 1 hour or overnight.

Place chicken on an oven tray and pour melted butter or margarine over. Cover with foil. Place in the oven and bake for 30 minutes.

Add tomato wedges and bake for another 30 minutes. Grill for 10–12 minutes uncovered until brown.

Serve with rice and salads.

Serves 4–6

Note: This recipe has no tandoori spice, but the spices used create a tandoori–like flavour. Use a mortar and pestle to combine spices.

TRADITIONAL CHICKEN CURRY
Simply divine

- 1 kg whole chicken, cut into pieces
- 1 large onion, finely chopped
- 30 ml oil
- 20 ml ginger and garlic paste
- 30 ml turmeric
- 15 ml jeera powder
- 20 ml koljana powder
- 5 ml cayenne pepper
- 15 ml red leaf masala
- 3 cardamom seeds
- 2 cinnamon sticks
- 10 ml salt
- 500 ml warm water
- 8 curry leaves
- finely chopped fresh dhania

Wash and drain chicken and keep aside. Sauté onion in heated oil over medium heat until soft and golden, adding water when necessary.

Add chicken, ginger and garlic, and sauté until chicken has absorbed the flavour; about 5 minutes.

Mix all spices with 100 ml water and add to pot. Simmer gently until well blended. Add rest of water and simmer until chicken is completely cooked, adding more water only if necessary.

During the last 5 minutes of cooking time, add curry leaves to infuse the dish. Stir in dhania. On serving, garnish with sprigs of dhania.

Serve with fluffy white rice or fried roti, poppadums, onion and tomato salad, atchar and golden potatoes.

Serves 6–8

Grilled whole tandoori chicken

GARLIC CHICKEN CASSEROLE
Served with a mushroom sauce

- 1 whole chicken, cut into pieces
- 45 ml garlic paste
- 45 ml chicken spice
- 10 ml paprika
- 5 ml white pepper
- 10 ml salt
- 60 ml oil

Sauce
- 30 ml oil
- 1 large onion, chopped finely
- 1 punnet mushrooms, sliced
- 3 medium tomatoes, grated
- 15 ml tomato purée
- 15 ml mixed herbs
- 5 ml black pepper
- 5 ml salt
- 60 ml parsley, chopped

Wash and drain chicken pieces. In a large bowl, mix chicken with spices and salt and marinate for 2 hours.

Preheat oven to 180 °C. In a large pot, add oil and brown chicken for 5–7 minutes, a few pieces at a time, taking care not to break chicken pieces.

Make the sauce in a separate pot. Braise onion and add mushrooms, tomatoes, purée, herbs and spices. Cook for 3 minutes. Add parsley and mix together well.

In an oven–proof dish, layer chicken and pour mushroom mixture over. Bake for 20–30 minutes till cooked.

Serve with white rice and salad.

Serves 6–8

CHICKEN A LA KING
Succulent chicken and crunchy veggies in a creamy, tangy sauce

- 1 kg chicken fillets, cubed
- 5 ml salt
- 5 ml black pepper
- 50 g butter
- 15 ml cooking oil
- 2 medium onions, chopped finely
- 1 large green pepper, cut into strips
- 1 large red pepper, cut into strips
- 1 large yellow pepper, cut into strips
- 3 medium carrots, cut into julienne strips
- 2 celery sticks, sliced
- 1 punnet mushrooms, halved
- 30 ml garlic paste
- 15 ml chicken spice
- 5 ml paprika
- 10 ml leaf masala
- 3 ml extra salt
- 500 ml fresh cream
- 20 ml cornflour

In a bowl, mix chicken with 5 ml salt and pepper. In a large pot, add butter, oil and chicken and stir–fry for 5 minutes, taking care not to burn chicken pieces. Remove and keep aside.

Add onions to same pot and sauté till golden, adding water if necessary, till onions are soft and pulpy. Add all vegetables and spices and stir–fry for 3 minutes.

In a clean pot, add chicken and vegetables. Mix together cream and cornflour, and stir into chicken mixture. Cook for 3 minutes. Switch off stove and leave pot on hot plate.

Serve with coconut sweet rice and roast potatoes.

Serves 6–8

Note: If a more saucy dish is required, add 60–100 ml water.

Garlic chicken casserole

Chicken

SEYCHELLES CREOLE CHICKEN RICE CASSEROLE
Simple, divine and finger–licking good

- 750 ml brown rice, uncooked
- 1 kg chicken portions, cleaned and drained
- 10 ml salt
- 10 ml black pepper
- 30 ml chicken spice
- 15 ml paprika
- 125 ml oil
- 30 ml crushed garlic
- 2 medium onions, chopped roughly
- 2 medium green peppers, cut into strips
- 1 tin whole peeled tomatoes
- 20 ml curry powder
- 2 ml dried thyme
- chopped dhania for garnish

Preheat oven to 180 °C. Cook rice in usual manner until done; rinse and allow to drain.

Season chicken with salt, pepper, chicken spice and paprika. Heat oil in a pot and brown chicken, a few pieces at a time, until cooked. Place chicken in shallow oven–proof dish and sprinkle rice on top.

In the same pot in which chicken has been cooked, place garlic, onions, green peppers, tomatoes, curry powder and herbs.

Cover with a lid and braise for 10 minutes. Season to taste if necessary. Spoon vegetables over rice. Cover with foil. Bake for 40 minutes until heated through and chicken is tender.

Garnish with fresh chopped dhania. Serve with veggies or salad of choice.

Serves 6–8

Seychelles creole chicken rice casserole

CHICKEN BREYANI
Chicken layered at the bottom, rice placed on top, then served side by side

Chicken layer masala
- 3 onions, finely chopped
- 45 ml cooking oil
- 4 medium tomatoes, grated
- 45 ml ginger and garlic paste
- 45 ml chicken masala
- 3 cardamom pods
- 2 pieces stick cinnamon
- 2 whole allspice
- 3 whole cloves
- 15 ml jeera powder
- 15 ml koljana powder
- 15 ml turmeric
- 3 green chillies
- 45 ml lemon juice
- salt to taste
- 1 kg chicken drumsticks
- 6 potatoes, cut into quarters

Rice layer
- 3 x 250 ml basmati rice, cooked
- 125 ml yellow lentils, cooked
- salt to taste
- 3 onions, sliced thinly and fried till golden
- ½ bunch fresh dhania, chopped
- 5 ml yellow food colouring mixed with 80 ml water (or a couple of strands of saffron) for sprinkling over rice
- butter

To make the chicken layer, braise the onions in cooking oil till soft, adding water if necessary. Add the other masala ingredients and braise for a few minutes.

Add the chicken and potatoes and cook for 30–45 minutes till done. Stir and check that masala does not burn. Take care not to break potato and chicken pieces.

To prepare the rice layer, add rice and salt to boiling water and cook till almost soft, taking care not to overcook. Set aside.

Cook the lentils and salt in boiling water and simmer till they are soft but still whole. Set aside.

Use enough oil to fry the onions till crispy and brown, but not burnt. It is best to fry them gently and slowly. Set aside.

To assemble the breyani, line the base of a large pot with a thick layer of foil. Add the chicken and potatoes to the pot. Place a cup of rice on top of the chicken. Coat another piece of foil with non-stick cooking spray and place the sprayed side onto the chicken layer. Place the rest of the rice on top of the foil, then place the lentils, onions and dhania on top of the rice.

Mix the yellow food colouring with the water and sprinkle over the rice. Top with pieces of butter and steam together for 20 minutes over low heat.

Serve by placing the rice mixture on one side of a big platter and the chicken masala on the other side. Serve with dhai (yoghurt and chutney) and freshly fried poppadums.

Serves 6–8

Chicken

CREAMY DHANIA BUTTER CHICKEN
A creamy dish with no tomato, but a lovely unusual colour

- 10 ml salt
- 5 ml yellow food colouring
- 1 kg chicken fillets, cubed
- 60 ml butter or margarine
- 15 ml cooking oil
- 1 medium onion, chopped finely
- 100 ml water

Chicken paste
- 30 ml jeera powder
- 30 ml koljana powder
- 15 ml cayenne pepper
- 5 ml turmeric
- 30 ml garlic paste
- 3 green chillies, chopped (optional)
- 50 ml water

Creamy dhania mixture
- 1 bunch dhania, cleaned
- 250 ml milk
- 30 ml cornflour
- 250 ml cream

Sprinkle salt and yellow food colouring over chicken and rub in well.

In a large pot, melt butter or margarine and cooking oil together. Braise chicken over low heat, a few pieces at a time. Remove from heat and keep aside; continue cooking till all pieces are braised.

In the same pot, add onion and 100 ml water. Cook onion till soft and transparent; it must be soft and mushy.

Place all chicken paste ingredients in a liquidiser and liquidise until smooth. Add to onion. Braise for 2–3 minutes till aroma rises.

Add chicken to spice and cook for 5–10 minutes till soft.

Meanwhile, liquidise dhania, cornflour and milk together and add to the chicken pot. Cook for 3–5 minutes. Remove from heat.

Pour cream into pot and stir well, taking care not to cook cream, as it will thin the sauce.

Serve with naan bread or white basmati rice.

Serves 6–8

Note: If sauce is too thin and a thicker consistency is required, add 15 ml cake flour to a little water and stir into a smooth paste. Add to pot before adding cream and allow to cook for a few minutes.

MOROCCAN CHICKEN
A tangy, sticky, Moroccan-flavoured dish

- 1 large chicken, cleaned and cut into pieces, drained
- salt to taste
- 5 ml white pepper
- 40 ml butter
- 30 ml oil
- 2 onions, thinly sliced
- 5 cinnamon sticks
- 3 whole cloves
- 15 ml turmeric
- 15 ml chicken spice
- 15 ml peri-peri powder
- 30 ml ginger and garlic paste
- 20 ml lemon juice
- 60 ml honey
- 100 g apricots
- 300 ml orange juice
- 200 g pitted dates, fresh or dry
- finely grated rind of 1 orange

Season chicken with salt and pepper. Heat butter and oil in a pot and brown chicken portions well.

Remove from pot, stir in onions and braise until golden. Add all remaining ingredients to pot except dates, chicken and orange rind.

Bring to the boil and then reduce heat. Add chicken, dates and rind to pot. Cover and simmer for 30–40 minutes.

Serve with yellow rice.

Serves 4–6

Note: It is important that the lid of the pot fits well. If not, place a layer of foil between lid and pot.

Morrocan chicken

CHAPTER SEVEN

Succulent Beef and Lamb

Luxuriously slow–cooked in
intriguing sauces: the use of
evocative spices and herbs
characterise the cooking of
most meat dishes. Delicious and
satisfying to every hearty appetite.

CREAMY CHOPS WITH SWEET POTATO
A delightful combination with a hint of curry

- 45 ml oil
- 1 kg chops
- 30 ml cake flour
- 5 ml salt
- 5 ml pepper
- 15 ml paprika
- 2 medium onions, finely chopped
- 20 ml curry powder
- 10 ml brown mustard seeds
- 30 ml crushed garlic
- 4 tomatoes, grated
- 500 g sweet potatoes, cut into large chunks
- 60 ml brown sugar
- salt to taste
- 90 ml dhania leaves, chopped
- 100 ml mayonnaise

Heat oil in a pot. Toss meat in flour, salt, pepper and paprika. Brown in pot over medium heat. Remove from pot and keep aside, covered.

Add onions to pot and simmer till soft, adding water if necessary. Stir in curry powder, mustard seeds and garlic. Cook for 2 minutes.

Add tomatoes, sweet potatoes, some water, sugar and salt. Bring to a slow boil, stirring often. Reduce tomato mixture by cooking for 10–15 minutes.

Mix dhania with mayonnaise. Add to tomato mixture, stirring gently. Place meat in a large square oven-proof dish and pour tomato mixture over. Bake for 15–20 minutes.

Serve with savoury rice and salad.

Serves 6–8

FILLED MEAT ROLL
Rolled like a Swiss roll and filled with creamy cheese and peppers

- 1 kg steak mince
- 3 medium carrots, grated
- 1 medium onion, grated
- 30 ml oil
- 2 slices stale white bread, soaked in water
- 3 eggs, beaten
- 100 ml chopped parsley
- 10 ml salt
- 10 ml black pepper
- 15 ml paprika
- 15 ml barbeque spice
- 15 ml crushed garlic
- 1 green pepper, coarsely grated
- 100 g coarsely grated cheese

Preheat oven to 180 °C. Line a loaf pan with lightly oiled foil.

Sauté onion and carrots in oil. Crumble the bread slices, draining excess water, and combine with meat, eggs, parsley, spices and onion mixture. Combine well.

Roll meat mixture onto a piece of plastic or foil to form a rectangle of about 40 cm x 30 cm.

Sprinkle meat with green pepper and cheese and roll up like a Swiss roll, using foil as a guide. Place roll in the loaf tin and bake, covered, for about 1 hour at 180 °C. Open foil covering and allow top to brown, basting with the sauce that has collected in the tin.

Remove from tin, allow to rest for 5 minutes and serve with sweet yellow rice, salad and veggies.

Serves 6–8

Note: If lots of sauce has collected in loaf pan, pour out into a small pot and cook to reduce to a thick sauce. Pour over meat roll when serving.

Creamy chops with sweet potato

TANDOORI LAMB, SPINACH AND ALMOND CURRY
A spicy, delectable dry curry

- 1 kg lamb, cut into small pieces
- 60 ml cooking oil
- 30 ml butter
- 3 medium onions, finely sliced
- 45 ml ginger and garlic paste
- 30 ml koljana powder
- 60 ml jeera powder
- 30 ml tandoori spice
- 15 ml whole coriander seeds
- 30 ml brown sugar
- 5 ml salt to taste
- 6 fresh curry leaves
- 2 green chillies, finely chopped
- 3 medium, firm tomatoes, grated
- 250 ml whole almonds
- 1 bunch spinach, shredded

Clean, wash and drain meat.

In a large heated pot, add oil and cook meat, stir-frying for 10–15 minutes. Add 150 ml water and cook till soft. Lower heat.

In a separate pot, melt butter and braise onions till soft and pulpy, adding water when necessary. Add all spices, sugar, salt, curry leaves, chillies and tomatoes, and simmer for 5–7 minutes.

Add tomato mixture to meat pot and stir well; cook for 5 minutes. Stir in almonds and spinach, place lid on pot to sweat for a few minutes and remove from stove.

Serve with flat breads or coconut rice.

Serves 6–8

LAMB CHOP AND BUTTERNUT CASSEROLE
Simply divine

- 25 ml cooking oil
- 1 kg lamb chops
- 10 ml salt
- 10 ml black pepper
- 10 ml dried thyme
- 15 ml cayenne pepper
- 10 ml sugar
- 2 medium onions, sliced
- 125 ml parsley
- 1 butternut, cut into large chunks
- 1 can mushroom soup, mixed with 100 ml water
- 250 ml fresh cream
- 250 ml cheese, grated
- grated cheese and chopped parsley for garnishing

In a large pot, add oil and heat. Sprinkle chops with spices and brown in hot oil. Remove and keep aside. Add onions and sauté. Add a little water to soften the onions.

Add meat, parsley and butternut to pot. Mix thoroughly and cook for 5–7 minutes. Place in an oven-proof dish. Pour mushroom soup over meat mixture. Cover with foil and bake in a moderate oven for 30–40 minutes.

Remove foil; pour cream over, sprinkle with grated cheese and return to the oven until cream is absorbed and cheese is melted and bubbly.

Sprinkle lightly with extra grated cheese and chopped parsley.

Serve with yellow rice and a crisp green salad.

Serves 6–8

Tandoori lamb, spinach and almond curry

MEAT BREYANI
Traditional breyani steamed in the oven

Rice
- 750 ml basmati rice, uncooked
- 2 cinnamon sticks
- 3 cloves
- 3 whole allspice
- 3 cardamom pods
- 60 ml oil
- 20 ml salt

Meat sauce
- 2 onions, finely chopped
- oil to sauté onions
- 1 kg meat, washed, trimmed and drained
- 20 ml garlic and ginger paste
- 2 green chillies
- 2 pieces stick cinnamon
- 3 cardamom pods
- 3 whole cloves
- 3 whole allspice
- 30 ml koljana powder
- 15 ml turmeric
- 10 ml jeera powder
- 10 ml barishap powder
- 15 ml cayenne pepper
- 15 ml garam masala
- 1 large tomato, grated
- 250 ml plain yoghurt
- 125 ml bunch fresh dhania, chopped

For layering
- 5 ml saffron, soaked in 60 ml boiling water
- 14 small whole potatoes, fried in oil
- 250 ml crispy golden fried onions
- 125 ml cooked lentils
- 125 ml melted butter

Prepare rice first. In 2 litres of water, boil rice and spices, oil and salt until rice is three–quarters done; firm, but just cooked. Rinse and drain rice well; put aside until required.

For the meat sauce, heat oil in a large pot. Add onions and sauté until golden. Add meat, ginger and garlic and sauté for 20 minutes, adding water if necessary.

Add all spices and tomato; cook till soft. Lastly add yoghurt and fresh dhania. Cook for a further 10 minutes until sauce is reduced.

Assemble
Using an oven–proof dish, place a layer of rice at the bottom, then a layer of meat sauce, followed by a layer of potatoes, lentils and fried onions. Repeat the process until all rice and meat is used, ending off with rice.

Sprinkle the top layer of rice with saffron water, melted butter, lentils and onions. Cover with foil and place in the oven at 180 °C and allow to steam until heated through.

Serve with dhai (yoghurt and chutney), onion salad and atchar.

Serves 8–10

Meat breyani

MAVROU
A traditional dish

- 10 ml salt
- 30 ml ginger and garlic paste
- 15 ml jeera powder
- 15 ml koljana powder
- 10 ml barishap powder
- 15 ml crushed red chillies
- 3 cloves
- 3 whole allspice
- 3 cardamom pods
- 3 cinnamon sticks
- 1 kg cubed steak or goulash
- oil for braising onions
- 4 large onions, thinly sliced
- 45 ml sugar
- 2 large tomatoes, grated
- few strands saffron

Combine all spices and mix well with meat. Marinate for an hour or overnight.

Heat oil in a large pot and braise onions until soft and golden, adding water when necessary and sprinkling sugar over onions while braising.

Add meat and cook, covered, until soft, adding water when necessary. Simmer slowly over low heat. Add tomatoes and continue to simmer.

Add saffron to 60 ml boiling water and allow to stand. Add saffron water to pot and allow to simmer for a few more minutes. Stir.

Garnish with finely chopped dhania. Serve with white or savoury rice.

Serves 6-8

MEAT AKNI
An easy way to serve curry

- 20 ml cooking oil
- 2 large onions, finely chopped
- 1 kg lamb or mutton pieces (or thick rib)
- 1 green chilli, finely chopped
- 15 ml salt, or to taste
- 15 ml ginger and garlic paste
- 15 ml jeera powder
- 15 ml koljana powder
- 5 ml barishap powder
- 15 ml turmeric
- 15 ml cayenne pepper
- 1 whole clove
- 3 cardamom seeds
- 3 cinnamon sticks
- 4 medium potatoes, peeled and quartered
- 100 ml hot water
- 4 x 250 ml uncooked rice
- 60 ml chopped dhania

Heat oil in a large pot. Add onions and braise until golden and soft.

Add meat and spices and cook covered over medium heat until meat is tender.

Add potatoes and water and cook for another 10 minutes.

Pour over rice; add enough water to cook rice. Fast-boil rice without stirring.

When settled, stir well and steam, covered, for 20-30 minutes or until rice is done.

Garnish with dhania and serve with atchar and dhai.

Serves 6-8

Note: This is an easy way to serve curry and rice as all the ingredients are cooked in one pot, so that the rice becomes moist and takes on the flavour of the curry

Mavrou

ROAST GARLIC LEG OF LAMB WITH LEMON POTATOES
A fusion of roasted garlic, lemon and orange with a flavour of fresh herbs

- 2 kg leg of lamb
- salt
- 10 cloves of garlic
- 100 ml fresh dhania stalks and leaves
- 60 ml butter or margarine
- 250 ml water
- 45 ml cake flour

Marinade
- 60 ml cooking oil
- rind of 2 lemons
- 2 lemons, juiced
- 2 oranges, juiced
- 15 ml black pepper
- 30 ml Portuguese spice
- 10 ml Cajun spice
- 10 ml peri–peri powder
- 20 ml fresh thyme
- 30 ml salt

Lemon potatoes
- 15 medium potatoes
- 60 ml butter, melted
- 60 ml orange juice
- 60 ml lemon juice
- 30 ml crushed garlic
- 30 ml black pepper
- 15 ml peri–peri powder
- grated lemon rind

Trim excess fat off lamb. Remove all glands and pat dry. Rub salt over leg. Using the point of a knife, make 10 incisions evenly over the top of the lamb (in the same direction that it will be sliced) deep enough to hold a clove of garlic and a dhania stalk.

Mix all marinade ingredients together well. Pour marinade over lamb and cover. Refrigerate overnight or at least for a couple of hours, turning occasionally.

In an oven tray, melt butter or margarine till golden brown and bubbly, taking care not to allow it to burn (add 5 ml oil to prevent burning). Drain lamb, reserve the marinade.

Place meat in an oven tray and bake at 180 °C, uncovered, for 40 minutes, turning meat halfway through the cooking process, taking care that garlic does not fall out.

Prepare lemon potatoes by mixing all ingredients with potatoes. Add potatoes to tray and bake meat for a further 30 minutes, turning again (take care to keep garlic in slits). Remove all juices from the pan and add to marinade. Cover the oven tray with foil and bake meat for an additional 30 minutes, or till meat and potatoes are tender.

Meanwhile, cook marinade, adding 250 ml water mixed well with 45 ml cake flour, and cook till reduced. Keep warm and when needed, serve in a gravy boat.

Remove foil from lamb and bake, uncovered, for 10 minutes. Remove the lamb and grill potatoes for 5–7 minutes, or until golden.

Slice lamb and place potatoes around the roast. Using a little of the pan juices, drizzle over roast and sprinkle with fresh chopped dhania leaves.

Serve with yellow rice, salad and gravy.

Serves 10–12

Roast garlic leg of lamb with lemon potatoes

TOMATO BREDIE
An old-fashioned firm favourite

- 40 ml cooking oil
- 8 cloves
- 2 large onions, thinly sliced
- 1 kg lamb or mutton pieces
- 5 ml ginger and garlic paste
- 5 ml salt
- 15 ml white pepper
- 60 ml sugar (optional)
- 2 green chillies
- 3 cups water
- 410 g can tomato purée
- 6 medium potatoes, cut into quarters
- 60 ml dhania leaves

Heat oil in a pot. Add cloves and onions; sauté until golden and soft.

Add meat and braise for 30 minutes or until meat is well browned, adding water if necessary.

Add garlic and ginger, salt, pepper, sugar and chillies. Braise, covered, with 3 cups of water.

Add tomato purée and stir well to blend. Add potatoes and cook for a further 15 minutes, or until potatoes are soft. Stir in dhania.

Serve with white rice and salads.

Serves 6-8

BEEF STROGANOFF
Simply a very good stroganoff

- 60 g butter
- 1 medium onion, thinly sliced
- 1 kg rump steak, cut into thin strips
- 200 g mushrooms, sliced
- 25 g cake flour
- 45 ml tomato purée
- 2 medium tomatoes, liquidised or grated
- salt to taste
- 5 ml white pepper
- 20 ml paprika
- 5 ml lemon pepper
- 15 ml peri-peri powder
- 250 ml sour cream or smetana

For garnishing
- chopped parsley
- tomato wedges

Melt half of the butter in a large pot. Fry onion until golden and soft, adding water if necessary. Remove with a slotted spoon.

Add rest of butter and melt. Add meat and sauté until brown. Remove with slotted spoon.

Add mushrooms and sauté for 2-3 minutes; remove from pan.

Stir flour into pan juices. Add purée, liquidised tomatoes and cook till smooth.

Add all seasonings and steak, onion and mushrooms; heat through thoroughly. Lastly add sour cream. Simmer to heat through.

To serve, place meat mixture on an oblong platter lengthwise, alternating with white rice. Garnish with finely chopped parsley and tomato wedges.

Serves 6-8

Tomato bredie

SESAME BEEF AND NUT MEDLEY
Serve as a very tasty light meal

- 30 ml cooking oil
- 500 g steak stroganoff (thin steak slices)
- 30 ml crushed garlic
- 1 green chilli, chopped
- 2 medium onions, sliced
- 30 ml lemon juice
- 30 ml soy sauce
- 5 ml brown sugar
- 30 ml chopped coriander leaves
- 100 g walnuts, roughly chopped
- 60 ml sesame seeds
- 5 ml lemon pepper
- 5 ml paprika
- salt to taste
- 1 cucumber, seeded and thinly sliced
- 1 green pepper, thinly sliced lengthwise
- 2 tomatoes, cut into quarters

Heat oil in a wok and cook meat over high heat for 8 – 10 minutes till meat is browned and all liquid has evaporated.

Add garlic, chilli and onions; cook for 2 minutes longer. Transfer meat to bowl and cover.

Combine lemon juice, soy sauce and sugar in a small bowl; pour over meat.

Stir in coriander leaves, nuts, seeds and spices. Add cucumber and green pepper.

Leave in fridge for about an hour for flavours to develop. Serve with tomatoes on a large platter with crusty bread.

Serves 4

SAVOURY TURKISH MUTTON PILAU
A rich dish, slightly spicy with a tantalising flavour

- 60 g butter
- 500 g mutton, coarsely chopped
- 1 onion, finely chopped
- 500 ml rice, uncooked
- 1 large tomato, peeled and chopped
- 50 ml seedless raisins
- 100 ml dried apricots
- 10 ml salt and pepper
- 20 ml barbeque spice
- 20 ml paprika
- 20 ml sage
- 3 whole allspice
- 100 ml orange juice
- rind of 1 orange
- water as required
- dhania for garnish

Heat butter and add meat; brown well. Add a little water to soften meat as it cooks. Simmer until completely soft. Remove meat from pot.

Add onion and sauté until soft and golden, adding water as needed.

Add rice and stir–fry for 5 minutes over moderate heat. Add meat, tomato, dried fruit, salt, spices, orange juice and enough water to cook rice.

Simmer over low heat until rice is tender and all liquid is absorbed; about 30 minutes. Sprinkle the orange rind over the rice.

Leave rice, covered, on stove top with plate switched off for about 15 minutes. Sprinkle with chopped dhania before serving.

Serves 4–6

MASHED POTATO STEAK PIE
Creamy mashed potato served with spicy steak strips

Mashed potato
- 1 kg large potatoes, peeled
- 30 ml butter
- 100 ml milk
- 15 ml garlic paste
- salt to taste
- freshly ground black pepper to taste

Steak filling
- 1 kg steak strips
- 15 ml paprika
- 30 ml Cajun spice
- 15 ml barbeque spice
- 10 ml garlic and ginger paste
- 15 ml oil
- 1 large onion, sliced finely
- salt to taste
- 60 ml butter, cut into blocks
- 60 ml chopped dhania

Mashed potato
Boil potatoes in salted water until soft. Pour off water, add butter and mash using a potato masher.

Add milk and garlic; place pot over gentle heat and reheat, stirring to prevent potato from burning. Add salt and pepper to taste. Add more milk if needed. Remove from heat and set aside, covered.

Steak filling
Marinate the steak overnight in spices. Heat oil in a large pot. Add onion and sauté until golden, adding water when necessary to soften the onion.

Add meat and braise until all water has evaporated. Add salt. Cook meat over medium heat, adding water when needed, until tender. When meat is soft, evaporated as much liquid as possible so that only a thick sauce remains.

Place meat in an oven–proof dish and spoon mash over it. Dot with pieces of butter and sprinkle with dhania.

Place in an oven that has been preheated to 180 °C and brown mash until golden.

Serve hot with salad.

Serves 6–8

Beef and Lamb

NIPPY SAUSAGE 'FULL OF FLAVOUR'
A quick delectable hot meal

- 250 ml fresh dhania leaves, chopped roughly
- 30 ml crushed garlic
- 10 ml lemon juice
- 60 ml cooking oil
- 1 kg nippy beef spicy sausage (separate at tie)
- 2 medium onions, sliced thinly
- 250 g mushrooms, halved
- 1 red pepper, sliced into long strips
- 15 ml paprika
- 15 ml coarse black pepper
- 60 ml Worcestershire sauce
- 30 ml cornflour, mixed with 100 ml water

Mix together dhania leaves, garlic, lemon juice and 30 ml oil in a bowl. Add sausage, coating well with the marinade. Leave aside for 15 minutes.

In a large pan, stir–fry sausage. Remove from heat and keep aside, covered.

In a large wok, add rest of oil and braise onions till soft and golden. Add mushrooms, pepper slices, paprika and black pepper.

Mix Worcestershire sauce into cornflour mixture. Add to wok; stir–fry for 2 minutes.

Add sausage to wok and mix in well with the mushroom mixture, heating through thoroughly.

Remove from heat, serve directly onto plates and accompany with crusty bread and salad.

Serves 6–8

LAMB WITH SAVOURY GREEN BEANS
A delicious way of simmering whole green beans in chilli sauce

- 45 ml cooking oil
- 1 kg lamb pieces, washed
- 3 medium onions, quartered
- 500 g green beans, trimmed
- 10 ml yellow mustard seeds
- 30 ml crushed garlic
- 2 red chillies, chopped
- 5 ml sugar
- 10 ml paprika
- 3 whole peppercorns
- 10 ml sesame seeds
- 10 ml jeera powder
- 30 ml lemon juice
- salt to taste

Sauce
- 15 ml cooking oil
- 45 ml soy sauce
- 60 ml honey
- 15 ml lemon juice
- 5 ml white pepper

In a large pot, add oil and brown meat over low heat until tender, about 25 minutes, adding water bit by bit, if necessary. Remove from pot and leave aside until required.

Add onions and beans to the pot, and stir–fry for 8–10 minutes.

Add all other ingredients to pot and stir–fry for 2–3 minutes. Toss in meat and heat through.

Combine all ingredients for the sauce, add to meat mixture and cook until sauce is well amalgamated with the meat.

Serve with sweet yellow rice.

Serves 6–8

Nippy sausage 'full of flavour'

TANGY MINCE BOBOTIE
An old-time favourite

- 3 slices white bread, crust removed
- 250 ml milk
- 45 ml cooking oil
- 2 medium onions, chopped
- 45 ml garlic paste
- 30 ml jeera powder
- 30 ml curry powder
- salt to taste
- 5 ml white pepper
- 10 ml Cajun spice
- 1 kg steak mince
- 15 ml brown sugar
- 10 ml turmeric
- 60 ml fruity chutney
- 100 g sultanas (optional)
- 15 ml grated lemon rind
- 3 eggs
- 200 ml fresh cream
- 2 ml grated nutmeg
- 30 ml chopped fresh parsley

Preheat oven to 180°C. Soak bread in a shallow bowl with milk.

Heat oil in a large pot; add onions and cook for 5–7 minutes till golden brown. Add garlic, jeera, curry powder, salt, pepper and Cajun spice. Cook, stirring, for 3 minutes; add steak mince and mix in well. Cook for 5–7 minutes.

Squeeze out bread, reserving milk. Mix bread, sugar, turmeric, chutney, sultanas, rind and salt to taste. Beat in 1 egg. Mix well with mince.

Transfer to a square casserole dish and bake for 30–45 minutes. Whisk together reserved milk, cream, remaining eggs, nutmeg and parsley.

Pour over top of mince mixture and bake for 20 minutes, or until topping is golden.

Serve with green salad.

Serves 8–10

LEMON AND BBQ CHOPS
Tangy and succulent

- 1 kg leg chops
- 10 ml paprika
- 30 ml lemon pepper
- 30 ml barbeque spice
- 10 ml salt
- 5 ml white pepper
- 50 ml chutney
- 30 ml Worcestershire sauce
- 45 ml chilli sauce
- 60 ml lemon juice
- oil for frying

Marinate chops with all spices, chutney, Worcestershire sauce, chilli sauce and lemon juice. Leave for 1–2 hours or overnight.

Heat oil in a large saucepan. Add chops one at a time (be careful; the oil will splatter).

Fry chops for 3–5 minutes on each side, until done. Place on absorbent paper to drain excess oil.

Serve with yellow rice and chunky vegetables.

Serves 6

Lemon and BBQ chops

FILLET STEAK WITH MUSHROOM SAUCE
Rich, creamy and simply so satisfying

- 1 kg whole fillet, cleaned and trimmed
- 5 ml salt
- 5 ml black pepper
- 60 ml oil for frying

Mushroom sauce
- 30 ml oil
- 1 medium onion, finely chopped
- 30 ml crushed garlic
- 1 punnet mushrooms, sliced
- 250 ml fresh cream
- 30 ml flour, mixed with 100 ml water
- 10 ml salt
- 5 ml black pepper

Cut fillet at 3–cm intervals. Sprinkle fillet with salt and pepper.

Heat oil in a large saucepan and fry fillet until it is cooked through. Set aside.

Sauce
Heat oil in a saucepan and sauté onion until soft and golden. Add garlic and mushrooms and sauté for 5 minutes.

Add cream, flour mixture, salt and pepper. Allow to cook until sauce thickens. Pour sauce over the cooked fillet.

Serves 6–8

MEATBALLS IN TOMATO SAUCE
A 'must have' with spaghetti or fluffy white rice

Tomato sauce
- 30 ml cooking oil
- 2 large onions, thinly sliced
- 410 g can tomato purée
- 410 g can water
- 10 ml crushed garlic
- 5 ml salt
- 10 ml white pepper
- 2 green chillies, finely chopped
- 4 cloves
- 4 peppercorns
- 30 ml sugar

Meatballs
- 500 g steak mince
- 1 green chilli, chopped
- 60 ml fresh dhania, chopped
- 5 ml white pepper
- 5 ml salt
- 10 ml crushed garlic
- 2.5 ml grated nutmeg
- 60 ml bread crumbs, or 2 slices bread soaked in water
- 1 egg

To make the sauce, heat oil in a large saucepan and braise onions until golden.

Add tomato purée, water and spices and simmer for 15 minutes. Stir in sugar till well blended and simmer for a further 5 minutes.

Combine all meatball ingredients and mould into small ping pong–size balls. Add to tomato mixture and cook for 15 minutes, or until meatballs are cooked through.

Serve with spaghetti or white rice.

Serves 6–8

Fillet steak with mushroom sauce

DENNINGVLEIS
The traditional version

- 2 large tomatoes, grated
- 15 ml ginger and garlic paste
- 20 ml crushed chillies
- 30 ml curry powder
- 8 whole allspice
- 15 ml salt, or to taste
- 15 ml freshly ground black pepper
- 4 curry leaves
- 4 bay leaves
- 15 ml sugar, or to taste
- 10 ml lemon juice
- 30 ml brown vinegar
- 1 kg leg of mutton; or mutton or lamb pieces
- 60 ml oil
- 3 large onions, thinly sliced
- ½ bunch fresh dhania leaves
- 2 fresh green chillies

Combine the tomatoes, spices, salt and pepper, curry leaves, bay leaves, sugar, lemon juice and vinegar well. Marinate meat or an hour.

Heat oil and sauté onions till golden and soft, adding water if necessary. Onions must be soft and mushy.

Add meat and cook, covered, over medium heat, adding water to prevent meat from drying out. Cook till gravy is thick and meat is soft.

Add dhania and chillies; cook for a few minutes further and serve.

Serve with vegetables and sweet rice.

Serves 6–8

LAMB CURRY
A classic meat curry

- 30 ml melted butter
- 30 ml cooking oil
- 2 large onions, finely sliced
- 1 piece stick cinnamon, broken
- 2 cloves
- 2 allspice pods
- 2 cardamom pods
- 1 kg lamb pieces (washed and drained)
- 45 ml garlic and ginger paste
- 2 medium tomatoes, liquidised or grated
- 10 ml salt
- 15 ml barishap powder
- 15 ml jeera powder
- 30 ml cayenne powder
- 15 ml turmeric
- 30 ml koljana powder
- 1 cup water

For garnishing
- fresh chopped dhania
- green chillies

Heat butter and oil in a pot. Add onions, cinnamon, cloves, allspice and cardamom.

Braise onions till well browned. Add meat and ginger and garlic paste. Cook for 20 minutes.

Add tomatoes, salt and spices. Cook till meat is tender. Add 1 cup of water and simmer for 10 minutes.

Garnish with fresh dhania and whole green chilli. Serve with roti or rice.

Serves 6–8

Variation: Add 4 medium potatoes, cut in half, when adding tomato.

Lamb curry

CHAPTER EIGHT

Home-Baked Breads

Nothing tastes quite as good as
fresh homemade bread. There is
something very satisfying about
slicing into a crusty loaf or breaking
a pan-fried roti.
Mouth-watering, distinctive,
delightfully tempting and baked
to perfection. The aroma is
sensational.

RABIA'S NAAN BREAD
My favourite naan bread

- 30 ml oil
- 60 ml sugar
- 30 ml butter or margarine, melted
- 5 ml salt
- 1 egg, beaten
- 375 ml lukewarm milk
- 4 x 250 ml cake flour
- 10 ml fennel seeds or whole aniseeds
- 1 packet instant dry yeast
- fennel, white poppy or sesame seeds for sprinkling

Preheat oven to 180°C and prepare a round cake tin.

Cream oil, sugar, butter or margarine and salt well. Add egg and milk. Mix well. Sift the flour in a separate bowl. Add fennel seeds or aniseeds. Sprinkle with yeast and mix through.

Add liquid mixture to flour; mix into a soft dough. Knead for 15–20 minutes, until dough is smooth and elastic. Leave dough in a large bowl to double in volume.

Divide mixture into 2. Shape each half into a sausage and cut into equal-sized pieces.

Shape pieces of dough into a round roll. Shape the dough as follows: with the piece of dough on the work surface, cup the dough with the palm of your hand. Do not lift dough from surface. Now gently roll dough with the palm of your hand in an anti-clockwise direction until a smooth well-shaped roll is obtained. Repeat this technique with the rest of the dough.

On completing the shaping of the rolls, place them next to one another in a prepared round tin. Brush with beaten egg and sprinkle with seeds. Leave to double in size.

Bake for 20 minutes, or until cooked through. Remove from the oven, allow to rest for 5 minutes and turn out from cake tin.

Makes 12–15 rolls

RABIA'S MILKY ROLLS
An easy basic dough for plain breads, filled breads and rolls

- 1 kg cake flour
- 30 ml sugar
- 10 ml salt
- 1 packet instant dry yeast
- 60 g butter, melted
- 15 ml oil
- 1 egg, beaten
- about 500 ml lukewarm milk

Topping
- beaten egg, for brushing
- sesame seeds

Sift flour, salt and sugar together; add yeast and run your fingers through the flour.

Mix together butter, oil, beaten egg and lukewarm milk; stir well. Add to dry ingredients, a little at a time, and mix well (do not add liquid all at once, or else the dough will be too soft). Knead well for about 15 minutes.

Place the dough into a large, oiled bowl. Cover with plastic wrap and leave to rise in a warm place until doubled in size.

Punch down the dough and form into desired shapes. Place in prepared oven trays and leave to rise for 15 minutes. Brush with egg wash and sprinkle with sesame seeds.

Bake in a preheated oven at 180°C for 15–20 minutes, or till an inserted skewer comes out clean. Turn out and cool on wire rack.

Makes 20–24

TUNA AND CHEESE TWISTED LOAF
A delectable filled spiral bread

Filling
- 200 ml grated cheese
- 15 ml chopped dhania
- 10 ml fish spice
- 10 ml crushed garlic
- 1 can tuna, drained and flaked
- 5 ml paprika

Dough
- 500 g cake flour
- 7 ml salt
- 10 g instant dry yeast
- 50 ml oil
- 350 ml lukewarm water

Topping
- beaten egg
- 200 ml cheese
- paprika for sprinkling

Prepare filling first by combining all the ingredients together and mixing well. Set aside until required.

To make the bread, sift flour and salt together. Add dry yeast and mix through with your fingers. Add oil to lukewarm water and pour into flour mixture. Mix to a soft dough. Turn onto a lightly oiled surface and knead well until smooth and elastic, about 15 minutes.

Place dough in an oiled bowl, pat top of dough with oil; cover with cling wrap and rest for 20 minutes.

Knock down the dough and roll out into a rectangle of 30 cm x 35 cm. Spread filling onto dough. Roll up like a Swiss roll, seal ends off well and then twist each end in opposite direction.

Place on a prepared baking tray. Snip dough across top a couple of times at regular intervals with kitchen scissors. Brush top with beaten egg, sprinkle with cheese and paprika. Allow to rise for 20–30 minutes, then bake at 180 °C for 30–40 minutes.

Serve with green salad or pasta.

INDIAN ROTIS
A soft pan-fried bread to serve with curries

- 750 ml cake flour
- salt to taste
- 60 ml melted butter
- 200 ml boiling water
- 100 ml milk
- 125 g butter, to rub onto roti
- some melted butter for frying

Sift flour and salt together.

Make a mixture of butter, boiling water and milk. Pour over flour mixture. Allow to cool.

Knead into a soft dough. Cover with a clean cloth and keep for 30–60 minutes before rolling.

Roll out as follows: roll out the complete ball of dough into a big roti. Spread with butter and sprinkle with flour. Roll up like a Swiss roll.

Squeeze dough with hands to distribute butter. Cut into pieces of desired size and pinch to seal. Let balls rest for 10 minutes.

Roll out each ball on a lightly floured surface to approximately 6 mm thickness.

Place on a hot dry griddle and turn over several times until lightly freckled.

Brush with melted butter in–between turning. Continue until all rotis are made, stacking the completed ones on top of one another.

Makes 12–15

CHICKEN AND SUNDRIED TOMATO WALNUT TWIST
Crisp, crunchy and mouth-watering

- 4 x 250 ml cake flour
- 90 ml sugar
- 5 ml salt
- 10 g instant dry yeast
- 80 g butter or margarine
- 10 ml grated orange rind
- 2 large eggs, beaten
- 50 ml fresh orange juice
- about 150 ml lukewarm water

Filling
- 2 medium onions, finely chopped
- 60 ml oil
- 2 chicken fillets, chopped
- 10 ml garlic, finely crushed
- 100 g walnuts, roughly chopped
- 30 ml chutney of choice
- 10 ml cayenne pepper
- salt to taste
- 100 ml sundried tomatoes, chopped into small pieces

Topping
- beaten egg
- poppy seeds

Mix flour, sugar and salt. Add yeast and mix.

Rub butter or margarine into flour with your fingertips. Add orange rind and mix.

Add beaten egg, juice and enough lukewarm water to make a soft dough. Knead the dough well for 10 minutes, or until smooth and elastic.

Place dough on a lightly floured surface, cover with greased cling wrap and leave to rest till doubled in bulk; knock down dough.

Meanwhile, make the filling. Sauté the onions very slowly in oil, adding water as required; cook until soft and golden. Add chicken and braise till done.

Add garlic, walnuts, chutney, seasonings and chopped sundried tomatoes. Stir-fry for 2 minutes. Set aside until required.

Divide dough into 2 equal pieces and roll each piece into a rectangle of 25 cm x 40 cm. Spread filling evenly over each rectangle. Roll each rectangle up into a Swiss roll, starting with the wide side. Twist the rolls around each other and pinch ends together well. Place on a prepared baking tray. Brush with beaten egg and sprinkle with poppy seeds.

Leave to rise until doubled in volume, about 45–50 minutes. Bake for 30–35 minutes in a preheated oven at 180 °C or until an inserted skewer comes out clean. Cool on a wire rack.

Makes 1 twist

Chicken and sundried tomato walnut twist

HONEY–ALMOND SEED LOAF
A 'must' with hearty soup

- 125 g cake flour
- 400 g nutty wheat flour
- 20 ml poppy seeds
- 50 g flaked almonds
- 5 ml salt
- 10 g instant dry yeast
- 60 g butter or margarine, cut into blocks
- 50 ml honey
- 350 ml lukewarm water
- beaten egg for brushing

Mix flour, nutty wheat, poppy seeds, almonds and salt together. Add yeast and mix through with your fingers.

Rub butter or margarine into flour mixture to resemble coarse breadcrumbs.

Stir honey into water and add to flour mixture. Knead into a soft pliable dough for about 15 minutes.

Place in a greased bowl and cover with cling wrap. Leave to rise in a warm place until doubled in bulk, about 45 minutes.

Knock dough down and place in a prepared loaf tin. Brush top with beaten egg and sprinkle with extra poppy seeds. Leave to rise for a further 45 minutes.

Bake for 20–30 minutes at 180 °C, or until done. Serve with a hearty soup.

Makes 1 loaf

THREE–SEED RAISIN BREAD
A seedy health bread

- 30 ml honey
- 600 ml lukewarm water
- 500 g whole–meal flour
- 120 g cake flour
- 5 ml salt
- 100 ml sunflower seeds
- 50 ml sesame seeds
- 50 ml poppy seeds
- 60 ml raisins
- 1 packet instant dry yeast

Topping
- beaten egg
- extra seeds

Coat a medium loaf pan with non–stick cooking spray.

Mix honey with warm water and stir to dissolve.

Mix flours, salt, seeds and raisins; sprinkle with yeast and mix through with your fingers.

Add honey liquid to flour mixture and mix into a soft dough. Add extra water as needed. Take care not to add too much water. Place onto an oiled surface and knead till soft and pliable, about 15–20 minutes.

Pat into prepared loaf tin. Brush with egg wash and sprinkle with seeds. Leave to rise to the top of the tin.

Carefully place the loaf tin in the oven and bake for 30 minutes at 200 °C. Continue baking at 180 °C for a further 30 minutes. Loosen sides and turn onto a wire rack to cool.

Cover with a damp cloth for softer bread, if desired.

Makes 1 flat–topped seeded loaf

Three-seed raisin bread

FOCCACIA
Sensationally savoury

- 500 ml cake flour
- 2.5 ml salt
- 1 packet instant dry yeast
- 10 ml mixed herbs
- 10 ml chopped fresh parsley
- 30 ml olive oil
- 250 ml warm water
- 1 small onion, finely chopped
- rosemary sprigs
- coarse salt for sprinkling (optional)
- 15 ml extra olive oil

Prepare 2 x 24-cm round pans. Sift flour and salt together. Add yeast and mix. Add herbs and run your fingers through to blend. Add oil and water and mix into a soft dough.

Turn onto a lightly oiled surface and knead into a smooth and elastic dough.

Place dough onto prepared trays. Cover dough with oiled cling wrap and let rest until doubled in volume.

Remove wrap and sprinkle lightly with onion and coarse salt. Decorate with a few rosemary sprigs. Drizzle with extra olive oil and bake at 200 °C for 25 minutes.

Let cool on a wire rack. Cut into wedges.

Makes 2 round flatbreads

CLASSIC SEED BRAN RING LOAF
A popular bread, and so versatile

- 400 g whole-meal flour
- 10 ml salt
- 5 ml sugar
- 1 packet instant dry yeast
- 100 ml sunflower seeds
- 50 ml linseeds
- 300 ml lukewarm water
- 30 ml oil

Line a ring pan with baking paper and coat well with non-stick cooking spray. Keep aside.

In a large bowl, sift whole-meal flour with salt. All the bran that is left in the sieve must be added to the bowl. Add sugar and mix through.

Sprinkle yeast over flour and run your fingers through to mix well. Add all seeds and mix into flour mixture.

Make a well in the centre of the mixture. Mix together lukewarm water and oil and pour into well, a little at a time, mixing to create a soft loose dough. As water is poured into well, stir all the time. Beat in bowl till smooth.

Pour dough into pan, cover with cling wrap and leave at room temperature until the mixture has doubled in size. Bake at 200 °C for about 1 hour, or until done.

Turn the bread out onto a wire rack and allow to cool. Serve with hot soup or fresh salads.

Makes 1 loaf

Foccacia

HERBED BREAD BRAID
Savoury bread with a herby taste

- 500 g cake flour
- 350 g bread flour
- 10 ml salt
- 10 ml sugar
- 2 packets instant dry yeast
- 25 ml melted butter
- 100 ml chopped parsley
- 5 ml dried thyme
- 1 small onion, finely chopped
- 10 ml crushed garlic
- 700 ml lukewarm water

Topping
- beaten egg
- 5 ml sesame seeds
- 30 ml ground almonds
- 60 ml cheese, finely grated

Prepare 2 oven trays. Sift both flours with salt and sugar. Sprinkle yeast over the flour mixture and run fingers through. Add butter, herbs, onion and garlic.

Pour liquid into a well in the flour; mix to make a workable dough (adding water as required).

Knead for about 15–20 minutes until smooth and elastic. Shape into a ball and place in an oiled bowl. Brush top of dough with a little oil.

Cover and leave to rise in a warm place until doubled in size.

Punch down; divide into two pieces. Divide each half into three; roll into long sausages and then plait, pinching to close at both ends.

Place loaves on prepared baking trays. Leave to rise until doubled in size.

Brush gently with egg and sprinkle with cheese, almonds and sesame seeds.

Bake for 10 minutes at 200 °C, then reduce heat to 180 °C and bake 20–30 minutes longer, or till done.

Serve with soup or salad.

Makes 2 braids

CRUSTY ONION LOAF
An unusual, sweet onion bread

- 3 eggs, beaten
- 60 ml condensed milk
- 15 ml oil
- 375 ml lukewarm milk
- 600 g cake flour
- 10 ml salt
- 1 packet instant dry yeast
- 125 ml onion slices, fried in a little oil

Topping
- beaten egg
- a few thin onion slices
- butter or margarine, melted

Preheat oven to 200 °C. Coat a large deep loaf tin or 2 small ones with non-stick cooking spray.

Combine eggs, condensed milk and oil. Mix well. Add warm milk and keep aside.

Mix flour and salt together. Sprinkle with yeast and run fingers through flour. Add fried onion. Mix into a soft pliable dough with the egg and milk mixture.

Knead on an oiled surface for 15–20 minutes. Place into an oiled bowl. Lightly pat top of dough with oil. Cover with cling wrap. Leave in a warm place for about 25–30 minutes.

Slightly press dough down. Roll into a rectangle to fit the loaf tin. Roll up like a Swiss roll. Take care that sides are the same thickness as centre. Neaten and place into loaf tin.

Brush lightly with egg. Sprinkle top with onion slices.

Place on middle shelf of oven and bake for 30–40 minutes, or till done. Remove from the oven and allow to stand for 2 minutes.

Turn out and gloss the sides and top of the loaf with a little butter or margarine. If soft crust is desired, wrap in a cloth and leave to sweat.

Serve as desired.

Makes 1 large or 2 small loaves

SPIRAL CINNAMON TEA BREAD
A crusty, layered tea bread filled with sweetness

- 1 kg cake flour
- 10 ml sugar
- 10 ml salt
- 2 packets instant dry yeast
- 2 eggs
- 100 g butter
- 600 ml lukewarm water
- 60 ml oil

Cinnamon sugar
- 200 ml brown sugar
- 60 ml ground cinnamon

Topping
- beaten egg

Prepare two cake tins or a tube pan. Sift flour, sugar and salt together. Mix in yeast and run fingers through flour mixture.

Beat eggs in a jug. Gently melt butter and add to milk. Add oil. Mix with eggs. Add liquid to flour and mix into a soft dough. Turn dough onto lightly oiled surface and knead for 15–20 minutes, until smooth and elastic.

Smear a large bowl with oil. Place dough inside and cover with cling wrap. Allow to double in volume in a warm place. Meanwhile, prepare cinnamon sugar by mixing cinnamon with brown sugar.

Punch dough down and form a sausage. Cut sausage into 20 equal-sized portions.

Take a portion and flatten it by tapping gently. Lay it on the bottom of the tin. Repeat this process until entire bottom is covered. Then sprinkle the layer with cinnamon sugar. Place a layer of flattened dough pieces on top of the sugar, then sprinkle with sugar again.

Continue layering until the tins are three-quarters filled. Brush with egg and sprinkle with sugar. Allow to rise until dough reaches the top of the baking tin.

Bake on middle shelf at 180 °C for 50–60 minutes, or until inserted skewer comes out clean. If you tap the bottom of the pan it must sound hollow. Turn onto a wire rack to cool.

Serve with butter and tea or coffee.

Makes 2 spiral loaves

ONION, GARLIC AND CASHEW SAVOURY RING
An onion–filled pull–apart ring topped with sweet-and-sour garlic cashews

Filling
- 45 ml butter or margarine
- 5 medium onions, finely sliced
- 15 ml lemon juice
- 100 ml water
- salt to taste
- 10 ml peri–peri powder
- 10 ml garlic paste
- 20 ml brown sugar
- 10 ml yellow food colouring

Dough
- 625 ml self–raising flour
- 5 ml black pepper
- 40 g butter or margarine
- 310 ml warm milk

Topping
- 10 cashews, roughly chopped
- 30 ml honey
- 5 ml lemon juice
- 20 ml butter or margarine
- 5 ml garlic, crushed
- 5 ml paprika

Prepare a 30–cm round tin. Preheat oven to 180 °C.

Make filling first. Heat butter or margarine in a small pot. Add onions and sauté until soft and glossy. Reduce heat; cover with a lid and allow to cook gently for a further 15 minutes until onions are very soft and have a golden colour.

Add remaining filling ingredients and simmer for about 15 minutes. Remove lid and cook for a further 10 minutes, stirring all the time, so that the onions caramelise; the filling must be moist–dry. Take care not to burn onions.

To make the dough, sift the flour into a bowl with black pepper. Rub in butter or margarine until mixture resembles fine breadcrumbs. Add enough milk to make a soft sticky dough.

Turn dough onto a lightly–floured surface and bring together by working gently till smooth and soft. Do not knead like a bread dough; it must have a glossy finish.

Roll dough out onto lightly–floured baking paper to a rectangle of 30 cm x 50 cm. Spread filling to within 3 cm of the long edge. Roll into a neat Swiss roll, taking care to guide dough so that filling stays within roll, starting from longest part of rectangle, using paper as a guide.

Place in fridge for 10–15 minutes. Use a floured serrated knife to cut roll into 16 slices. Place 14 slices upright around edge of pan and place remaining slices in centre.

Bake at 180 °C for 25–30 minutes. Stand for a few minutes and turn out onto wire rack to cool.

Make topping by mixing all ingredients together over a low heat. Brush savoury ring with warm topping.

Serve as a centrepiece or as a starter with salad.

Makes 1 ring

Onion, garlic and cashew savoury ring

CHILLI AND GARLIC LEBANESE FLAT BREAD

A delicately-flavoured flat bread to serve with curries

- 1 kg cake flour
- 10 ml salt
- 1 packet instant dry yeast
- 60 g butter or margarine
- 1 medium onion, finely chopped
- 45 ml crushed garlic
- 100 ml fresh dhania, finely chopped
- 1 green chilli, chopped finely
- 10 ml coarse black pepper
- 600 ml lukewarm water (or as required)

Sift the flour and salt together twice. Sprinkle with yeast and mix through with your fingers. Rub in the butter or margarine.

Add onion, garlic, dhania, green chilli and black pepper and mix through. Make a well in the centre and add three-quarters of the required water to the flour.

Mix into a soft pliable dough, adding more water if necessary. Knead dough for 10–15 minutes till soft and smooth. Place in a lightly oiled bowl and cover with cling wrap until doubled in size.

Roll dough into a long sausage and cut into 30–40 equal pieces. Roll pieces into long oblong shapes on a lightly floured surface.

Meanwhile, heat a flat pan over moderate heat. Fry bread till freckled, brushing with melted butter on each side. Transfer fried bread to a plate and keep covered until needed. Continue with rest of dough until all bread is prepared.

Serve with any curry dish as desired.

Makes 30–40 flat breads

PUREES (INDIAN FRIED BREAD)

- 500 ml cake flour
- 10 ml baking powder
- 5 ml salt
- 100 ml melted butter
- 60 ml oil
- 250 ml hot water (or as required)

Sift together flour, baking powder and salt. Add melted butter and oil and rub until flour resembles breadcrumbs.

Add enough water to make a soft dough. Knead well. Cover and allow dough to rest for 30 minutes.

Roll out thinly and cut with a round biscuit cutter.

Fry in hot oil. For purees to puff, scoop hot oil over them while frying. Fry until lightly golden.

Drain on absorbent paper.

Makes 20–30 breads

Chilli and garlic Lebanese flat bread

CHAPTER NINE

Sweet Treats

With a little imagination, even the simplest treat can become a gourmet offering. The secret is to choose complementary flavours, interesting textures and striking colours, elevating it from the common to the extraordinary.

DANISH PASTRIES
Pastries that will enchant your family

Pastry
- 500 ml cake flour
- 25 g butter or margarine
- pinch of salt
- 5 g instant dry yeast
- 1 egg, beaten
- 100 ml water
- 25 g castor sugar
- 150 g hard butter or margarine

Filling
- 1 can pie apples
- 60 ml brown sugar
- 60 ml raisins

Topping
- 1 egg, beaten
- 100 ml glacé icing

Sift flour and rub in 25 g butter or margarine. Add salt and mix through flour. Add yeast and mix well.

Mix together the egg, water and castor sugar. Add liquid to flour mixture; make a dough and knead until smooth. Cover and leave at room temperature for 15 minutes.

Cut 150 g butter into small squares. Roll dough into a square shape and place blocks of butter in the centre of dough. Fold dough like an envelope and seal the edges.

Place dough in the fridge for 30 minutes to rest. Roll out dough again; fold and return to fridge for another 30 minutes; roll and rest pastry a further two times. Make an arrow to indicate in which direction the pastry should be rolled. Only roll to the front. Cut pastry into squares.

Mix pie apples and raisins with brown sugar, making sure to cut all large pieces of apple into smaller pieces.

Place filling on one side of pastry. Fold over and press down sides, sealing with water. Take care to neaten edges. Cut two slits on top of pastry.

Brush with beaten egg and place on a prepared baking sheet. Bake in preheated oven at 200 °C for 20–30 minutes. Cool and drizzle with glacé icing.

Makes 18–20

Variation: Use custard or canned peaches to fill pastries, and fold in different decorative ways.

COCONUT MERINGUE TARTLETS
A beautiful tartlet with a jam filling and meringue topping

Pastry
- 375 ml cake flour
- 125 g butter, cut into small blocks
- 1 egg yolk
- 50 ml iced water
- 100 ml apricot or strawberry jam

Meringue
- 4 egg whites
- 250 ml castor sugar
- 250 ml desiccated coconut

Spray tartlet pans with non-stick cooking spray.

Sift dry ingredients into a bowl. Add butter and rub in until mixture resembles breadcrumbs. Add egg yolk and water and mix to form a stiff dough. Cover with cling wrap and chill for at least 30 minutes before using.

Roll out pastry to about 3 cm thickness. Using a round biscuit cutter, cut into circles that are slightly larger than those of the pans, to allow for shrinkage. Press pastry into pan moulds. Place a little jam in each.

Beat egg whites until stiff. Gradually add castor sugar and continue beating till stiff peaks form and mixture turns glossy. Gently fold in coconut.

Spoon meringue mixture over the jam to cover it completely.

Bake in a preheated oven at 200 °C for 15–20 minutes, until meringue is slightly browned. Remove and cool on a wire rack.

Makes 12–15

PECAN SHORTBREADS
Simply divine and nutty

- 230 g butter
- 50 ml icing sugar
- 500 ml cake flour
- 25 ml cornflour
- 5–10 ml lemon juice or water
- 125 ml chopped pecan nuts, processed
- whole pecan nuts for decorating
- icing sugar for dusting

Preheat oven to 180 °C. Keep aside an ungreased baking tray.

Cream butter and sugar until light and fluffy. Add sifted dry ingredients and work slowly. Add the liquid and finally the nuts.

Roll into small balls and press a whole pecan firmly on top. Bake for 15–20 minutes.

While still warm, dust biscuits with icing sugar.

Makes 36–40

LITTLE CUPCAKES
A kid's delight

- 250 g butter
- 575 ml sugar
- 6 eggs
- 500 g self–raising flour
- 125 ml cake flour
- 10 ml baking powder
- 250 ml milk

Topping
- butter icing or glacé icing
- 100s and 1000s

Preheat oven to 180 °C. Place colourful paper cups in muffin trays or small tartlet trays.

Cream butter and sugar until light and fluffy. Add eggs one at a time. Sift in flours and baking powder, alternating with milk, and fold in well.

Fill paper cups halfway and bake for 10–12 minutes, or until lightly golden and springy to the touch. Remove to a wire rack and cool.

When cool, decorate with icing and sprinkle with 100s and 1000s.

Makes 36

Little cupcakes

SNOWBALLS
Moist, soft and light

- 250 g butter
- 575 ml sugar
- 6 eggs
- 500 g self–raising flour
- 125 ml cake flour
- 10 ml baking powder
- about 250 ml milk

For rolling
- apricot jam, smoothed and softened with boiling water
- desiccated coconut, coloured as required

For filling
- whipped cream

Preheat oven to 180 °C and coat muffin or snowball trays with non–stick cooking spray.

Cream butter and sugar together until light and fluffy. Add eggs one at a time, beating until smooth.

Sift in flours and baking powder, alternating with milk, and fold in well.

Pour equally into moulds and bake for 10–12 minutes, or until lightly golden and springy to the touch. Remove to a wire rack and cool.

Dip snowballs in warmed jam and then in coconut. Allow to set. Cut in half and pipe with fresh cream.

Makes 36–40

PEACH TARTLETS
Layered pastry with a fruity, creamy filling

- 1 kg ready-made puff pastry
- 1 beaten egg
- cornflour for rolling
- 410 g can peach slices, drained
- 200 ml caramel
- 250 ml fresh cream, whipped
- icing sugar for sifting

Preheat oven to 200 °C. Prepare baking sheets by spraying with non-stick cooking spray.

Cut pastry in half; keep one half in refrigerator. Sprinkle working surface with cornflour.

Roll pastry out to 5–7 mm thickness, taking care not to let pastry stick to the surface. Using a large scone cutter, cut pastry into rounds.

Place on prepared tray. Brush top with beaten egg. Repeat process with other half of the pastry.

Bake at 200 °C for 7 minutes; lower heat to 180 °C and bake until golden. Remove from trays and place on a cooling rack.

When cooled, lightly open the centre of rounds, pipe in some caramel and cream and place two peach slices into each pastry.

Sprinkle with icing sugar and serve.

Makes 20 pastries

CUSTARD KISSES
Crunchy, tasty and quick to make

- 125 g butter or margarine
- 125 ml castor sugar
- 2 egg yolks
- 180 ml cake flour
- 180 ml self-raising flour
- 80 ml vanilla custard powder

Butter cream
- 40 g butter or margarine, softened
- 160 ml icing sugar, sifted
- 15 ml milk

Preheat oven to 180°C. Spray baking trays with non-stick cooking spray.

Using an electric beater, beat butter or margarine and sugar until light and creamy. Add egg yolks one at a time, beating thoroughly after each addition. Sift in flours and custard and fold in with a metal spoon until ingredients are just combined and the mixture is almost smooth.

Press mixture to form a soft dough. Roll one level teaspoon of mixture at a time into small balls. Arrange on baking sheet 5 cm apart. Flatten lightly with the base of a glass to a 2.5 cm round.

Bake for 12 minutes, or until lightly golden. Cool on a wire rack.

Make butter cream by beating butter with a wooden spoon until smooth. Sift in icing sugar. Gradually add milk, stirring until combined and smooth. Spread icing over one biscuit and place another on top. Repeat until all biscuits completed.

Store in an airtight container.

Makes 36–40

Note: Dough mixture can be cut out with a cookie cutter for a decorative variation.

GINGER NUTS
Just like grandma used to bake; crunchy and crispy

- 230 g butter or margarine
- 200 g sugar
- 250 ml golden syrup
- 50 ml ground ginger
- 10 ml bicarbonate of soda
- 12.5 ml milk
- 525 g cake flour

Preheat oven to 180 °C and spray a baking sheet with non-stick cooking spray.

Mix butter, sugar, golden syrup and ginger together. Mix bicarbonate of soda with milk and stir into butter mixture. Add flour and mix thoroughly.

Roll dough into small balls and place them apart on the baking sheet. Do not flatten balls.

Bake biscuits for 12–15 minutes, or until golden brown. Remove from oven and loosen from baking sheet.

If a very crunchy biscuit is required, switch off oven and leave biscuits to harden further.

Makes 36–40

CHOCOLATE PUFFS
Chocolate biscuits with a filling and dipped in chocolate vermicelli

- 230 g butter or margarine
- 50 ml icing sugar
- 450 ml cake flour
- 50 ml cocoa powder
- 25 ml cornflour
- 5–10 ml water
- icing sugar for dusting
- chocolate vermicelli for decoration

Butter icing
- 80 g butter or margarine
- 300 g icing sugar

Preheat oven to 180 °C. Keep aside an ungreased baking tray.

Cream butter and sugar until light and fluffy. Add sifted dry ingredients and work together slowly.

Add the liquid and mix into a soft dough. Roll into small balls and press tops lightly with a fork. Bake for 15–20 minutes. Allow to cool on a wire rack.

To make the icing, cream the butter well. Gradually add icing sugar. As the mixture thickens, add a little liquid (milk or water) to make a smooth spreading consistency.

Spread a layer of icing on one biscuit. Place another biscuit on top. Spread the sides of the two biscuits (now forming one) with icing and roll sides in chocolate vermicelli. Lastly, dust with icing sugar.

Store in an airtight container.

Makes 36–40

COCONUT CITRUS SYRUP CAKE
Moist and wickedly sweet

- 125 g butter
- 200 ml castor sugar
- 4 large eggs
- 500 ml desiccated coconut
- 250 ml self-raising flour

Syrup
- 30 ml lemon juice
- 125 ml fresh orange juice
- 150 ml sugar

Topping
- grated orange peel or grated fresh coconut

Preheat oven to 180 °C. Line base of a 20 cm ring pan with greasproof paper and spray with non-stick cooking spray.

With an electric mixer, cream butter and sugar in a bowl until light and fluffy.

Beat in eggs one at a time until well combined and smooth. Stir in coconut and lastly sift in flour.

Spread mixture into the prepared pan. Bake for 30–35 minutes; if cake is still moist in the centre, cover with foil and bake till done.

Meanwhile, in a small pot, combine ingredients for the syrup; stir over medium heat without boiling until sugar dissolves. Slowly bring to the boil, reduce heat and simmer, uncovered, for 3 minutes.

Pour hot syrup over hot cake and decorate with orange peel or grated coconut.

Yields 8–10 slices

BLUEBERRY CHEESECAKE
Divine and more-ish

Base
- 1 packet tennis biscuits, finely crushed
- 130 g butter, melted

Filling
- 500 g creamed cottage cheese
- 200 ml cream
- 160 ml castor sugar
- 15 ml lemon juice
- 4 eggs

Topping
- 375 ml sour cream
- 45 ml sugar

To decorate
- 100 ml blueberry jam
- 1 punnet blueberries

Preheat oven to 180 °C. Line base of a 24 cm springform tin with baking paper and spray with non-stick cooking spray.

Mix butter and biscuit crumbs together well. Spoon biscuit mixture into tin, pressing firmly onto base and sides. Refrigerate until firm.

Beat cottage cheese until smooth. Add cream; blend in well. Add sugar and lemon juice; beat till smooth. Add eggs one at a time, beating well in between. Pour mixture over crust and bake for 40 minutes, or until firm.

Mix topping ingredients together and spoon over baked cake. Bake in oven for a further 15 minutes; switch oven off and leave in oven for a further 30 minutes to set.

Melt jam in the microwave and add blueberries. Pour blueberry mixture over cheesecake, and allow to thicken slightly.

Serves 6–8

Coconut citrus syrup cake

DELECTABLE CHOCOLATE BROWNIES
Chocolate and nuts combine in lip–smacking goodness

- 375 ml cake flour
- 60 ml cocoa powder
- 5 ml baking powder
- 2.5 ml bicarbonate of soda
- 125 ml macadamia nuts, chopped
- 125 g butter
- 200 g dark chocolate, chopped
- 250 ml castor sugar
- 2 eggs, lightly beaten
- 80 ml sour cream

Topping
- 200 g dark chocolate, melted
- 100 g butter
- 100 g icing sugar
- 80 ml extra chopped macadamia nuts for sprinkling

Preheat oven to 180 °C. Prepare a 23 cm square tin. Line base and sides with greaseproof paper. Spray with non–stick cooking spray.

Sift flour with cocoa, baking powder and bicarbonate of soda into a large mixing bowl. Add nuts. Make a well in the centre.

Place butter and chocolate in a heat–proof bowl. Stand over a pan of simmering water and stir until chocolate is melted and mixture is smooth. Remove from heat.

Add castor sugar, eggs and sour cream to chocolate; beat with wire whisk until ingredients are well combined, thick and smooth.

Add chocolate mixture to dry ingredients, a little at a time, using a spatula, until ingredients are well combined. Do not over–mix.

Spread into prepared tin and bake for 30–40 minutes, or until inserted skewer comes out clean. Cool in tin.

To make the topping, place melted chocolate in a bowl; stir in butter and icing sugar until well blended.

Spread topping over the cooled brownie mix. Decorate with chopped nuts. Once topping has set, cut into squares.

Makes 16 squares

Note: Topping may be reheated, if necessary, to spread more easily.

DEVONSHIRE CREAM CAKE
Decadent, creamy and dreamy

- 100g cake flour
- 50g cornflour
- pinch of salt
- 5 extra–large eggs, separated
- grated rind and juice of 1 lemon
- 200g castor sugar, divided in half

Filling
- 250ml whipping cream
- 75g icing sugar

Topping
- 40g cocoa powder
- 100g icing sugar
- boiling water

Preheat oven to 180°C. Lightly coat a savarin mould with non–stick cooking spray.

In a bowl, sift together flour, cornflour and salt twice. In a separate bowl, beat egg yolks, lemon rind and juice until fluffy and light, gradually beat in half the sugar.

Continue beating until mixture is thick and creamy. Add flour mix and fold in gently.

Beat egg whites till stiff but not dry. Gradually beat in remaining castor sugar. Fold egg whites into egg yolk mixture.

Pour into prepared cake tin and bake for 40–45 minutes, or until a skewer inserted comes out clean. Remove from oven and leave to rest for 5 minutes; turn out onto a cooling rack to cool down completely.

Make filling by beating together cream and icing sugar until thick.

Slice cake through horizontally. Sandwich cake halves together with cream.

Sift together cocoa and icing sugar. Mix with boiling water into a fairly runny glaze. Allow glaze to stand and thicken somewhat. Pour over cake, allowing glaze to drip down the sides of the cake.

Serves 8–10

Note: 40–45 minutes baking time may be too much for this cake, so check after 30–35 minutes.

CARAMEL WALNUT CAKE
An exotic, rich classic walnut cake

- 230 g self–raising flour
- 2 ml baking powder
- 230 g butter
- 230 g castor sugar
- 4 large eggs
- 125 ml milk
- 50 g chopped walnuts

Filling
- 90 g butter or margarine
- 180 g icing sugar

Topping
- 50 g butter
- 60 g soft brown sugar
- 12 ml golden syrup
- ½ tin condensed milk
- 25 g milk chocolate
- 25 g chopped walnuts (for decoration)

Preheat oven to 180 °C and prepare two loose–bottomed 19 cm round tins with non–stick cooking spray.

Sift self–raising flour and baking powder twice. Cream butter and castor sugar together well. Beat in eggs one at a time until smooth.

Add flour to the creamed mixture, alternating with the milk until well blended. Mix walnuts in with the last of the flour; mix well.

Divide batter equally between tins, making a slight 'well' in the centre of each cake (not right to the bottom of the pan; just scoop the batter a little to the sides).

Bake in the oven for 20–25 minutes till an inserted skewer comes out clean. Remove from oven; cool for 2–5 minutes and remove from the pan and cool on a wire rack.

Make filling by creaming butter and icing sugar together till light and creamy. Sandwich cakes together.

Prepare topping. Heat butter, sugar, syrup and condensed milk over low heat, stirring continuously, till golden caramel in colour. Remove from heat and add chocolate, stirring till the chocolate melts. Top cake with warm mixture and sprinkle with chopped walnuts.

Serves 8–10

Caramel walnut cake

CHOCOLATE MOUSSE CAKE
Heavenly delicious, rich and creamy

- 4 large eggs
- 130 g cake flour
- 30 g cocoa powder
- 200 g sugar
- 15 ml baking powder
- 125 ml oil
- 125 ml water

Chocolate mousse filling
- 200 g dark chocolate
- 75 ml milk
- 12.5 ml gelatine
- 25 ml water
- 4 eggs, separated
- 250 ml cream

Cocoa cream
- 250 ml fresh cream
- 15 ml cocoa powder
- 20 ml icing sugar

Chocolate ganache
- 200 g dark chocolate, melted
- 155 g tinned cream

Preheat oven to 180 °C. Line two 22 cm springform cake tins with greaseproof paper and spray with non-stick cooking spray.

Separate eggs, placing whites in a large clean mixing bowl. Place egg yolks in a small bowl. In another clean bowl, sift all dry ingredients together. Add oil and water. Beat for 2 minutes. Add egg yolks and beat for a further 2 minutes.

Whisk egg whites until stiff and fold into chocolate batter with a spatula. Pour into cake tins and bake for 20–25 minutes or until firm to the touch and a skewer comes out clean. When cold, cut each cake into 2 horizontally.

Mousse filling
Break chocolate into a bowl. Melt chocolate over simmering water. Do not stir until chocolate has completely softened. Test with the tip of a teaspoon. Stir in milk. Meanwhile, sprinkle gelatine over water. Microwave on medium until gelatine is just melted. Add to chocolate, stirring as you do this.

Beat egg yolks until pale yellow. Pour in chocolate. Beat cream until stiff. Beat egg whites until stiff, but not dry. Add both to chocolate mixture and fold in gently with a spatula. Refrigerate for 10 minutes.

Meanwhile, place fresh cream in a clean bowl. Sift icing sugar and cocoa over. Whip cream until stiff. Line the base of one of the baking tins with baking paper. Place a cake layer in the baking tin and spread with mousse. Then place a layer of cake on top. Then spread with a layer of cream. Top with cake, then mousse, then cream. End off with cake. Place in fridge for at least 3–4 hours and allow mousse to set.

Make ganache by mixing chocolate and tinned cream together. Pour ganache over cake and spread smooth. Allow to set. Decorate with rose petals and chocolate curls.

Serves 8–10

Chocolate mousse cake

SUMMER FRUIT PAVLOVA
**Meringue with a marshmallow–like centre
topped with delectable fresh summer fruit**

- 5 egg whites
- 250 ml castor sugar
- 15 ml cornflour
- 5 ml white vinegar

Filling
- 250 ml cream, whipped or
  mascarpone cheese

Topping
- strawberries, kiwi fruit, berries,
  passion fruit, or any fruit of choice

Preheat oven to 140 °C. Cover an oven tray with baking paper and mark a 20–cm circle on paper. Spray well with non–stick cooking spray.

Beat egg whites in a stainless steel or glass bowl with electric beater until soft peaks form. Gradually add castor sugar; beat until dissolved between additions. Fold in cornflour and vinegar. Meringue should be glossy at this stage.

Spread meringue over baking paper and shape into a circle, using a small spatula to level the meringue. Swirl spatula, making an indentation in the middle of the meringue.

Bake for about 1 hour, thereafter reduce temperature to 100 °C and bake for a further 5–10 minutes.

Turn oven off and leave meringue to cool completely in oven, leaving door ajar.

Remove baking paper carefully; set aside until required. Meringue can be kept in an airtight container for a day or two.

When ready to serve, whip cream or cheese and fill meringue centre. Decorate with fruit of choice.

Serves 6–8

LEMON MERINGUE PIE

The tang of the lemony filling and the sweetness of the meringue combine deliciously in this rich dessert

Pastry
- 45 ml butter
- 100 g castor sugar
- 1 large egg
- 125 g cake flour
- 5 ml baking powder

Filling
- 1 tin full cream condensed milk
- 2 extra-large egg yolks
- grated rind of 2 medium lemons
- juice of 3 medium lemons

Topping
- 6 extra-large egg whites
- 75 g castor sugar
- 40 g icing sugar, sifted

Preheat oven to 190 °C. Spray a 20-cm pie dish with non-stick cooking spray.

Cream butter and sugar together. Add egg and beat well. Sift together flour and baking powder. Fold into creamed butter mixture and beat until just combined. Press pastry into pie dish; bake blind at 190 °C for 12–15 minutes.

To make filling, combine all ingredients, mixing well. Pour into pre-baked pie shell and bake for a further 10 minutes at 190 °C.

Meanwhile whisk egg whites for topping until stiff. Add castor sugar a little at a time, beating constantly. Spoon meringue mixture onto the filling.

Return to oven and bake at 160 °C for a further 10–15 minutes, or until meringue starts to brown. Remove from oven and allow to cool.

Yields 8 slices

CRÈME CARAMEL
A light, baked custard with a liquid caramel topping

Custard
- 3 extra-large whole eggs
- 5 extra-large egg yolks
- 75 ml sugar
- 500 ml lukewarm milk
- 500 ml cream
- 1 ml yellow food colouring

Caramel syrup
- 250 ml sugar
- 60 ml water

Preheat oven to 150°C.

Whisk the whole eggs, egg yolks and sugar together until light and creamy.

Add the lukewarm milk, cream and food colouring and mix well.

Pour this mixture through a fine sieve into a bowl and then into small ramekin bowls.

Place the ramekins in an oven-roasting pan and add enough hot water to come halfway up the sides of the ramekins.

Bake for 30–40 minutes, or until a skewer inserted in the centre comes out clean. Important: the crème caramel may not look set at the centre as there will still be a lot of movement when the ramekin bowl is gently shaken, but as it cools it continues to set.

Remove the ramekins from the water and allow to cool completely; cover and refrigerate.

To make the syrup, place sugar and water in a heavy-based saucepan and stir well.

Heat over low heat without stirring until the sugar melts and changes to a golden brown colour; watch it carefully as it becomes bitter if allowed to get too brown. Allow to cool for 10 minutes.

To serve, dip the base of the ramekins into boiling water for about 2 minutes. Loosen the sides neatly. Turn each ramekin out onto a chilled dish and pour the syrup over the custard.

Serves 6–8

Créme caramel

DELICIOUS BROWN MALVA PUDDING
A sweet indulgence

Batter
- 250 g butter or margarine, softened
- 250 ml sugar
- 2 extra-large eggs
- 500 g self-raising flour, sifted
- 500 ml milk
- 25 ml white vinegar
- 10 ml bicarbonate of soda
- 2.5 ml salt
- 50 ml smooth apricot jam

Cream sauce
- 375 ml cream
- 375 ml milk
- 200 ml sugar
- 30 g butter

Preheat oven to 180 °C. Prepare an oven-proof dish.

Cream together butter and sugar until light and fluffy. Add eggs, one at a time, beating well after each addition.

Add flour and milk alternately to creamed mixture, beating well. Mix together vinegar, bicarbonate of soda, salt and jam. Stir into flour mixture.

Turn batter into the greased dish and bake for 40 minutes or until a skewer inserted in the centre comes out clean.

Combine all ingredients for the cream sauce in a large saucepan over medium heat; bring to the boil. Simmer for 2–3 minutes, stirring now and then.

When pudding comes out of the oven, prick well with a skewer or fork. Pour sauce over and allow it to soak in.

Serves 6–8

Hint: This dessert can be made in advance and frozen for up to three months, wrapped in cling wrap. Thaw overnight. Reheat.

CRUNCHY CREAMY LAYERED BREAD PUDDING
Traditional bread pudding made decadent with cream and coconut

- 8 large eggs
- 250 ml sugar
- 10 slices bread, crust removed
- 1 litre milk
- 5 ml yellow food colouring
- 250 ml desiccated coconut
- 250 ml fresh cream
- 10 cinnamon sticks
- 2 cardamom pods
- 100 ml margarine or butter, cut into small blocks

Preheat oven to 180 °C. Coat an oven-proof dish with non-stick cooking spray.

Beat eggs and sugar well.

Soak bread in milk until soft and liquidise until smooth and creamy. Mix with egg. Stir in food colouring, coconut and cream.

Pour into prepared oven-proof dish. Add cinnamon and cardamom; dot with butter. Bake for 30 minutes, or until set.

Cut into squares and serve with a dollop of cream or custard.

Serves 12–15

MACADAMIA NUT AND PINEAPPLE PUDDING
Lustrous, velvety, tangy and nutty

- 200 g butter or margarine
- 250 ml sugar
- 3 eggs
- 560 ml cake flour
- 15 ml baking powder
- 150 ml milk
- 250 ml desiccated coconut
- 125 ml macadamia nuts, chopped
- 2 x 440 g tins crushed pineapple
- 50 ml chopped macadamia nuts for sprinkling

Topping
- 50 g butter or margarine, melted
- 100 ml honey
- 250 ml cream

Preheat oven to 180 °C. Spray a square oven–proof dish with non–stick cooking spray.

Beat butter or margarine, sugar and eggs together. Sift the flour and baking powder together and add to egg mixture. Add in milk and beat together.

Add coconut, nuts and pineapple and mix well. Spoon into prepared oven dish.

Bake pudding for 30–40 minutes.

To make the topping, melt butter or margarine and honey together; add cream and bring to the boil to thicken slightly.

Pour over pudding as soon as it comes out of the oven and sprinkle with nuts; return to oven for 5 minutes.

Serve hot with custard or cream.

Serves 6–8

RASPBERRY AND STRAWBERRY DELIGHT
Fresh and light

- 1 packet raspberry jelly
- 250 ml boiling water
- 410 g can evaporated milk, chilled overnight
- 250 ml fresh cream
- 500 ml strawberry yoghurt
- 50 ml castor sugar

Topping
- 250 ml fresh cream, whipped (optional)
- fresh raspberries for decoration

Dissolve jelly in boiling water and cool.

Whip evaporated milk until thick and doubled in bulk; add the jelly and mix well.

Whip fresh cream separately and add to jelly mixture. Blend well. Add yoghurt and castor sugar and stir until thoroughly combined.

Pour into a mould or individual bowls and refrigerate until well set.

Decorate with rosettes of cream if desired and garnish with fresh raspberries.

Serves 6–8

CHOCOLATE MOUSSE
A delectable chocolate treat

- 250 g dark chocolate
- 3 eggs
- 60 g castor sugar
- 250 ml cream, whipped until soft peaks form

Place chocolate in a small heatproof bowl. Stir over a pan of simmering water until chocolate has melted and mixture is smooth. Set aside to cool.

Using an electric beater, beat eggs and sugar in a small bowl for 5 minutes or until thick, pale and increased in volume.

Transfer mixture to a large bowl. Using a metal spoon, fold melted chocolate into the egg mixture.

Fold in whipped cream. Work quickly and lightly until mixture is just combined.

Refrigerate for 2 hours, or till mousse is set.

Serves 6–8

Raspberry and strawberry delight

RAISIN AND OATMEAL MUFFINS
A classic breakfast or perfect midday snack

- 85 g oats
- 250 ml buttermilk
- 120 g butter, cut into blocks
- 100 g dark brown sugar
- 2 large eggs
- 120 g cake flour
- 10 ml baking powder
- 30 g raisins

In a medium–sized bowl, mix oats with buttermilk and allow to soak for an hour.

Preheat oven to 180 °C and coat 2 muffin trays with non–stick cooking spray.

In a separate bowl, cream butter and sugar together until light and fluffy. Add eggs one at a time and beat. Sift flour and baking powder, and mix into egg mixture alternating with oats mixture.

Fold in the raisins. Do not over–mix; the mixture must be lumpy.

Pour into muffin cups and bake for 20 minutes, or until an inserted skewer comes out clean. Cool on a wire rack.

Makes 12

GINGER DATE MUFFINS WITH CARAMEL SAUCE
A simply 'must be made' muffin with a creamy caramel sauce

- 250 ml chopped dates
- 80 ml water
- 5 ml bicarbonate of soda
- 500 ml self–raising flour
- 250 ml cake flour
- 10 ml ground ginger
- 2.5 ml mixed spice
- 250 ml firmly packed brown sugar
- 1 egg, lightly beaten
- 300 ml milk
- 60 ml oil

Caramel sauce
- 250 ml firmly packed brown sugar
- 250 ml fresh cream
- 40 g butter

Preheat oven to 200 °C. Spray 2 muffin trays with non–stick cooking spray.

Combine dates and water in a pan. Bring to the boil. Remove from heat and add bicarbonate of soda, allow to stand for 5 minutes.

Sift dry ingredients into a large bowl, stir in date mixture and remaining ingredients.

Spoon mixture into prepared muffin trays and bake 20 minutes.

Serve warm with caramel sauce.

Caramel sauce
Combine all ingredients in a small pot. Stir over low heat, without boiling, until sugar is dissolved. Simmer, without stirring, for 3 minutes. Remove from heat.

Makes 12–15

Raisin and oatmeal muffins

CHAPTER TEN

Classic Family Favourites

Flavourful, family favourites that
resonate with memories of home.
The secrets of many heart–warming
family favourites that are at once
classic, innovative and traditional.

SEERKHOMO
A traditional milk drink to serve on Eid mornings

- 60 ml sago
- 30 ml semolina
- 30 ml vermicelli
- 2 cardamom pods
- 3 cinnamon sticks
- 100 g butter
- 2 litres milk
- 5 ml yellow food colouring
- ½ tin of condensed milk
- 125 ml crushed or slivered almonds
- 60 ml coarsely chopped pistachio nuts
- 60 ml charoli nuts (optional)
- 250 ml fresh cream (optional)

Braise sago, semolina, vermicelli, cardamom and stick cinnamon over medium heat until semolina turns pink (take care not to burn the mixture).

Add butter and braise for a further 2–3 minutes.

Add milk, yellow food colouring, condensed milk and nuts. Cook until vermicelli has softened and mixture is creamy. Stir at regular intervals.

If a more creamy texture is required, add fresh cream and bring to a slow boil. For a thinner consistency, add more milk and bring to a slow boil.

Pour into fancy cups and serve hot.

Serves 6–8

SPECIAL CREAMY BOEBER
Served traditionally during religious festivities and on cold winter nights

- 60 g butter
- 200 ml vermicelli
- 3 cinnamon sticks
- 3 cardamom pods
- 100 ml sago
- 80 ml semolina
- 250 ml water
- 1.5 litres milk
- 1 tin condensed milk
- 1 tin evaporated milk
- 2 ml yellow food colouring
- 100 ml sultanas or raisins (optional)
- 70 g flaked almonds, toasted

In a medium-sized pot, melt butter over medium heat. Do not overheat.

Add vermicelli, cinnamon sticks and cardamom pods, and sauté until the vermicelli is lightly golden in colour, taking care not to burn the vermicelli.

Add sago, semolina, water and milk, stirring continuously, to prevent sago from sticking to the base of the pot.

Once milk mixture reaches boiling point, add condensed milk, evaporated milk and yellow food colouring. Simmer for 10 minutes on low heat until the boeber is thick and creamy.

Add toasted almonds and sultanas or raisins (if using) just before serving. Serve hot.

Serves 6–8

CREAMY CARAMEL DIAMONDS (DODERY)
A velvety, creamy pudding

- 2 litres milk
- 500 ml cornflour
- 60 ml golden syrup
- 250 ml soft brown sugar
- 10 ml cardamom powder
- 250 g butter or margarine
- white poppy seeds for sprinkling

Preheat oven to 180°C. Spray an oven–proof dish with non–stick cooking spray.

In a large pot with a thick base, mix together all ingredients, except butter and poppy seeds. Heat over moderate heat, stirring continuously.

When milk mixture is warm, add the butter. Continue to stir until mixture becomes custard–like, taking care not to burn mixture.

When mixture is thick and like caramel, remove from stove. Pour into the prepared dish and sprinkle with poppy seeds.

Bake in oven for 20–30 minutes, or till set. Remove from oven and cool completely. Cut into diamond shapes and serve.

Makes 24 diamonds or 30 squares

Note: The mixture must be completely cold before the diamonds are cut, or else it will still be too soft.

GAHZURI
Deliciously crunchy cardamom and semolina biscuits

- 6 eggs
- 700 g sugar
- 250 g butter or ghee, melted
- 125 ml milk
- 2 ml salt
- 20 ml fine cardamom powder
- 700 g semolina
- 700 g cake flour
- oil for deep frying

Beat eggs and sugar together well. Beat in melted butter or ghee, milk, salt and cardamom.

Add semolina and flour into mixture to form a stiff smooth dough.

Roll out dough and use a heart shape or round cookie cutter to cut out biscuit shapes.

Heat oil in a saucepan. Fry biscuits in deep oil until crispy and golden.

Makes 40–50 biscuits

Note: Due to the butter content in the biscuits, foam will develop in the oil. Change oil halfway through the frying process.

NAAN KHATAAI
Much–loved traditional buttery short bread biscuit

- 375 g butter or ghee, melted
- 2 ml nutmeg
- a few strands of saffron
- 2 ml salt
- 10 ml fine cardamom powder
- 800 ml cake flour
- 250 ml castor sugar
- 75 ml semolina
- 2 ml baking powder
- coloured whole almonds, for decoration

Mix butter or ghee with nutmeg, saffron, salt and cardamom. Sift all dry ingredients into butter and mix into a soft dough. Leave overnight in the fridge.

Preheat the oven to 180 °C and apply non–stick cooking spray to baking sheets.

Form small balls with the dough. Slightly cut a criss–cross in the dough with a sharp knife. Decorate with an almond.

Place on baking sheets, taking care to allow enough space between dough balls for them to spread.

Bake for 12 – 15 minutes until lightly golden.

Makes 36–40 rounds

POTATO KOEKSISTERS
Soft, spicy koeksisters dipped into syrup and rolled in coconut

Dough
- 4 medium potatoes
- 4 x 250 ml cake flour
- 5 ml salt
- 5 ml ground nutmeg
- 15 ml ground cinnamon
- 10 ml ground ginger
- 15 ml whole aniseed
- 5 ml fine aniseed
- 60 ml sugar
- 1 packet instant dry yeast
- 30 ml butter
- 250 ml warm milk
- 60 ml oil
- 1 egg, beaten
- coconut for rolling
- oil for deep frying

Syrup
- 500 ml sugar
- 300 ml water
- 2 cinnamon sticks

Boil potatoes and mash while still hot. Potatoes must be smooth (do not discard all water, keep about a third for mashing the potatoes to a soft consistency).

Sift flour with salt, spices and sugar. Sprinkle over yeast and mix through.

Melt butter. Add milk, oil and beaten egg. Mix well and add to potatoes.

Make well in centre of flour and add the warm milk mixture. Mix into a soft dough. Place on working surface and knead until soft, smooth and elastic. Knead for about 15 minutes. Place in a lightly oiled bowl. Lightly oil top of dough and cover with cling wrap. Place in a warm place to double in size.

On a lightly oiled surface, roll dough into a sausage. Cut into equal size portions and shape each portion like a koeksister. Leave on lightly greased surface to double in volume; about 15 minutes. Lift koeksisters gently and reshape or neaten if needed.

Fry in moderately heated oil until golden in colour on both sides.

Meanwhile, make the syrup. Simmer the sugar, water and cinnamon over low heat until syrupy.

Dip each koeksister in sugar syrup over low heat. Roll in coconut. Drain on wire rack and allow to cool.

Makes 36–40

Note: Take care that the oil is moderately hot so that koeksisters do not absorb oil.

Hint: Koeksisters can be frozen for up to 3 months before dipping. Thaw at room temperature and sugar as normal.

Potato koeksisters

ORANGE AND POPPY SEED MUFFINS
Light, tangy and scrumptious

* 120 g butter, cut into blocks
* 100 g sugar
* 2 large eggs
* 1 small tub of apricot yoghurt
* 250 g cake flour
* 10 ml bicarbonate of soda
* 2.5 ml baking powder
* 30 ml poppy seeds
* zest of 1 orange

Preheat oven to 180 °C and coat 2 muffin trays with non–stick cooking spray.

In a bowl, beat together butter and sugar till creamy. Add eggs one at a time and beat well. Mix in yoghurt.

Sift in dry ingredients, poppy seeds and orange rind. Swiftly mix together. Do not over–mix. If needed, add a little milk to the batter if it looks too stiff.

Divide between muffin cups and bake for 20 minutes, or until golden. Serve with butter and orange marmalade.

Makes 12

CHOCOLATE HAZELNUT MUFFINS
Decadently divine

* 625 ml self–raising flour
* 2 ml bicarbonate of soda
* 25 g cocoa powder
* 100 g firmly packed brown sugar
* 125 g butter, melted
* 2 eggs, lightly beaten
* 250 ml buttermilk
* 250 ml Nutella or Bar One spread

Preheat oven at 200 °C. Spray 2 muffin trays with non–stick cooking spray.

Sift dry ingredients into a large bowl.

Stir butter, eggs and buttermilk together. Mix into dry ingredients, taking care that all flour has been moistened.

Spoon mixture to a depth of about one–third in muffin cups. Top with 15 ml Nutella or Bar One spread, and spoon over more muffin mixture.

Bake in a moderately hot oven for about 20 minutes. Serve with a hot drink.

Makes 12–15

Orange and poppy seed muffins

Cooking AND Baking TERMS

ACCOMPANIMENTS: Items offered separately with a dish.

AGAR–AGAR POWDER: A vegetarian alternative to gelatine. It's dry seaweed and is used as a stabiliser.

AL DENTE: Pasta firm to the bite.

ALLSPICE: Small dark brown berry. The flavour resembles a blend of cinnamon, cloves and nutmeg.

ALMONDS: Nuts that can be bought with the skin on, blanched, whole, halved, flaked, chopped or ground.

ANISEED: This is a small seed with a liquorice flavour. Fennel seed is often used as a substitute for anise.

ARBORIO RICE: Thick, shorter grain of rice with a high starch content. Also known as risotto rice.

AU GRATIN: Sprinkled with breadcrumbs and cheese and browned.

BAIN–MARIE:
- A container of water to keep foods hot without fear of burning.
- A container of water for cooking foods to prevent them burning.
- A deep narrow container for storing hot sauces, soups and gravies.

BAKE BLIND: To bake a pastry shell before adding the filling. To prevent the base from puffing up or making the sides collapse, line a pie dish with pastry, prick the base with a fork. Cover with wax paper slightly larger than the dish and fill with dried beans. Bake at 200 °C for 15 minutes. Remove beans and paper. Ready to fill.

BASIL: Use sparingly. Clove–like flavour and goes well with tomato. Sprinkle over salads and tomato halves.

BASTE: To spoon melted fat or other liquid over meat while it is cooking in the oven to keep it moist.

BATTER: A mixture of egg, flour and milk with seasoning for coating fish, other foods, preparatory to frying; the same mixture of a thicker consistency is used to make flapjacks and fritters.

BAY LEAF: Aromatic with slightly bitter taste. Used in pickled fish, sosaties, denningvleis. Use sparingly. Discard leaves after usage.

BEAT: To blend a mixture until smooth, using a wooden spoon and a rapid circular movement to introduce air.

BÉCHAMEL: Basic white sauce.

BINDING: Adding liquid like eggs, cream or melted butter to dry ingredients to hold ingredients together to form a dough.

BLANCH: To immerse fruit or vegetables in boiling water briefly to stop enzyme action before cooling down and freezing.

BLEND: To combine ingredients until smooth, either by hand or in electric blender or food processor.

BOIL: To cook in liquid over high heat where large bubbles rise to the surface and burst.

BRAISE: To brown onions etc. in a little oil or butter over moderate heat.

BRINE: A preserving solution of water, salt, saltpetre used for meats, fish etc.

BROWN: To cook food until the surface becomes brown.

BRUISE: To crush ginger or garlic to release flavour.

BUTTER: To coat or brush the inside of a mould or dish with butter.

BUTTERMILK: Liquid remaining from the churning of butter.

CANAPÉ: A cushion of bread on which are served various foods, hot or cold.

CARAMELISE: To melt sugar in a heavey–based saucepan, stirring constantly to obtain a golden colour.

CARDAMOM: Lightly crushed for curries, breyanis and rice dishes. Ground elachi used for puddings, koeksisters, biscuits and cakes.

CASSEROLE: Fire–proof earthenware dish.

CAYENNE PEPPER: Cayenne pepper is ground from the flesh and seeds of chilli pepper. It looks quite similar to paprika, and is extremely hot.

CHILL: To refrigerate until ice cold.

CHOP: To cut roughly into pieces.

CIABATTA: Moist Italian bread made with olive oil.

CINNAMON: Aromatic bark of cinnamon or cassia trees. Has rich, spicy aroma with sweet flavour. Used in curries, breyanis, vegetables, puddings and desserts.

CLOVES: Dried flower buds of a tropical tree; pungent, sweet flavour. Used in savoury and sweet dishes.

COMPOTE: Stewed (stewed fruit).

CORIANDER: Both the fresh leaves and seeds are used. It's also called dhania or cilantro. Used for garnishing, flavouring curry dishes, savouries, samoosas.

CRÈME FRAICHE: Whipping cream and buttermilk heated to 24 –29 °C (75 – 84 °F).

CROUTONS: Fried bread, used as garnish. For soups, they are cut in small cubes, for other dishes in a variety of fancy shapes.

CRUDITÉS: Small neat pieces of raw vegetables.

CURDLE: When fresh milk, cream or yoghurt separates from over–heating or when adding eggs too quickly to a mixture.

CUT IN: To mix solid shortening with dry ingredients for baking, using two knives or a spatula; when making scones and pastries, to mix in liquid in the same way.

DEGLAZE: To add liquid to the juices in a pan after cooking, then stirring over heat, scraping off bits of meat and fat, preparing to making a sauce or gravy.

DROPPING CONSISTENCY: When the consistency of a mixture is neither stiff nor runny; slowly falls from a spoon.

EGG WASH: When a mixture of beaten eggs and milk is used to brush the top of pies, scones to give them a shine when baked.

EMULSION: A mixture of oil and liquid (such as vinegar) that does not separate on standing (mayonnaise).

FLAKE : To carefully break up cooked or canned meat, fish or chicken using a fork.

FOLD IN: To mix ingredients lightly and gradually, to incorporate air, in a figure–of–eight motion (lifting and turning), using a metal spoon or spatula.

FREEZER BURN: Affects frozen items which are spoiled due to being unprotected for too long.

GARAM MASALA: A mixture of ground spices; but the basic ingredients are cumin, coriander and turmeric. Makes food fragrant, rather than hot. Add to dish just before serving. Used in curries or breyanis.

GARNISH: Adding herbs or sprinkles to a dish on completion.

GHEE: The Indian name for clarified butter; ghee is pure butterfat.

GLAZE: To brush with syrup or egg before or while baking to give a shine to meat, breads or pastries.

GLUTEN: This is formed from protein in flour when mixed with water.

GRAM FLOUR: This flour is made from ground chickpeas. It has a pale yellow colour and is powdery with an earthy flavour.

HORS–D'OEUVRE: Appetising first course.

INFUSE: To gently heat or steep in order to extract flavour, usually from a vanilla pod etc.

JULIENNE: Cut into fine strips.

KNEAD: To stretch and fold dough ensuring even mixing of ingredients, particularly yeast–based mixtures.

LEMON GRASS: This root is available fresh, powdered or in a dried form. Commonly used in Thai and Asian cuisine. Used to flavour soups, curries, savoury fish dishes.

MARINATE: To tenderise meat, fish or poultry by allowing it to stand in a marinade usually containing oil, vinegar, lemon juice and herbs and spices.

MASCARPONE: A creamy, thick Italian cheese used in sweet and savoury dishes.

MENU: List of dishes available.

MERINGUE: Egg whites and sugar whisked until stiff.

MINT: A very strong aromatic herb, with two varieties: peppermint and spearmint. Used in lamb dishes, tea, punch, as garnish, desserts, sauces and salads.

NUTMEG: Also called mace. Its aromatic flavour enhances egg dishes. Also used in cakes and stews. It is used in milk and rice puddings. Also apple pies etc.

PETIT FOURS: Very small pastries, biscuits, sweets and sweet–meats.

POACH: To cook gently in water or milk just below boiling point.

POPPADUMS: Dried, thin, large round wafers made from lentil flour, used as an accompaniment to Indian dishes.

POPPY SEED: Tiny blue–black seeds with a faint but distinctive flavour. Used as garnish for breads.

PRALINE: Almonds and sugar cooked together until caramelised. Pour into a baking tray lined with greaseproof paper. Used to decorate cakes, etc.

PROVE: To allow to rise in a warm place, allowing raising agent, e.g. yeast, to expand dough to twice its size.

PULSES: Vegetables grown in pods (peas and beans) and dried; source of protein and roughage.

PURÉE: To mash and sieve or liquidise food, especially fruit and vegetables, until it becomes a smooth and thick liquid.

REDUCE: To boil vigorously, uncovered, so that the liquid in a dish becomes concentrated.

ROUX: Flour stirred into melted butter, used for thickening soups and sauces. It may be white or brown.

RUB IN: To mix butter or margarine or oil and flour together with the fingertips until the mixture resembles breadcrumbs, for example when making scones or shortcrust pastry.

SALMONELLA: Food poisoning bacterium found in meat and poultry.

SAUTÉ: To toss quickly in a pan with oil.

SEAL or SEAR: To brown the surface of meat quickly over high heat to seal in juices.

SEASON: To add salt and spices.

SET: To allow to become firm or firmer (jelly).

SHORTENING: The butter or margarine used in baking.

SHRED: To cut meat or vegetables into fine slices or strips.

SIMMER: To cook slowly in a saucepan with bubbles rising to surface occasionally.

SMETANA: A low–fat product; a cross between soured cream and yoghurt.

SOUFFLÉ: A very light dish, sweet or savoury, hot or cold.

SOY SAUCE: Made from soybeans and used extensively in Chinese cooking.

SPONGE: To soak yeast with liquid and a little flour to allow fermenting to take place. Needed for fresh yeast and active dried yeast, instant yeast does not require sponging.

STRAIN: To separate the liquids from the solids by passing through a strainer.

TAHINI: A sesame seed paste.

TOFU: Low–fat bean curd made from soybeans.

VEGAN: A person who does not eat fish, meat, poultry, game, dairy products and eggs.

VEGETARIAN: A person who does not eat meat, poultry or game.

WHIP: To beat vigorously in order to thicken, e.g. cream.

VOL–AU–VENT: A puffy pastry case.

WHISK: To beat rapidly with a wire whisk or electric beater to incorporate air, e.g. egg white.

WOK: A round–bottomed pan used extensively in Chinese cooking.

ZEST: Outer skin of citrus fruit, containing strong, fragrant oils. Usually finely grated and used for flavouring a variety of dishes and desserts.

Compiled by Rehana Parker

OF DOUGH MAKING FOR BISCUITS

Rubbing–in method

- Butter is added to flour and rubbed in with the fingertips until mixture resembles fine breadcrumbs.
- Use cold firm butter to prevent mixture from becoming too sticky.
- Handle dough lightly and as little as possible.

Creaming method

- Butter and sugar are creamed together to get a creamy and fluffy texture.
- Creaming can be done by hand, wooden spoon or electric mixer.
- Flour mixtures may be mixed in by hand but take care not to make the dough too soft or sticky.
- Refrigerate the dough rather than being tempted to add more flour, since the texture of the biscuits will be changed.
- Do not allow dough to become too hard in the fridge since this will make it difficult to roll and causes it to crack.

Whisking method

- Produces sponge–like biscuits and those that are crisp and wafer thin.
- Before flour is added, eggs and sugar are beaten together until they are thick.

Melting method

- Can produce crisp to hard biscuits.
- This type of dough tends to have a high sugar content and may be sticky when warm.
- When the dough cools it will become less sticky, so do not be tempted to add more flour.

No–bake biscuits

- Many of the mixtures are bound together with melted chocolate.
- Do not overheat chocolate when melting it and do not allow the water to splash into it since it will make the chocolate go grainy and thick.
- Never allow water to boil when melting chocolate; water should be kept at a gentle simmer.
- Tastes good when served slightly chilled.

Refrigerator biscuits

- Dough must be thoroughly chilled before cutting into slices for baking.
- These biscuits spread easily, so space well when baking.

BAKING READINESS

- Most biscuits will be lightly browned on top. They will be soft and will set when left to cool on a wire rack.
- Generally a product is baked when it leaves the sides of the pan (breads, cakes, buns). If bread is still slightly moist, remove from the pan and bake for an extra 10 minutes.
- A skewer inserted in the centre comes out clean.
- Bread released from the pan sounds hollow when tapped at the bottom.

BAKING TIMES CHART

The following are approximate times and temperatures for baking various products:

BAKING	TIME	TEMPERATURE	BAKING	TIME	TEMPERATURE
Biscuits	12 – 15 minutes	180 °C – 200 °C	Meringues	1 hour	120 °C
Breads (yeast)	50 – 60 minutes	180 °C	Muffins	20 – 25 minutes	200 °C
Cakes, fruit	2 – 4 hours	140 °C	Pastry shell	12 – 15 minutes	220 °C
Cakes, sponge	1 hour	160 °C	Quiche	25 – 30 minutes	180 °C
Cup cakes	20 – 25 minutes	180 °C	Quick breads (with bicarb)	45 – 60 minutes	180 °C
Layer cakes	25 – 30 minutes	180 °C	Rolls (yeast)	20 – 30 minutes	180 °C
Loaves	45 – 60 minutes	180 °C	Scones	10 – 12 minutes	200 °C
Milk tart	10 minutes	200 °C	Two–crust pie, cooked filling	25 – 35 minutes	200 °C
	then 10 – 15 minutes	at 180 °C	Two–crust pie, uncooked filling	30 – 45 minutes	200 °C
Meringue shells	10 – 15 minutes	180 °C			

Index

Index